T0365265

Praise and Worship

JL WILLIAMS

authorHOUSE

AuthorHouse™
1663 Liberty Drive
Bloomington, IN 47403
www.authorhouse.com
Phone: 833-262-8899

Published by AuthorHouse   07/29/2022

ISBN: 978-1-6655-6535-6 (sc)
ISBN: 978-1-6655-6534-9 (e)

Library of Congress Control Number: 2022913194

Print information available on the last page.

Dedicated to my beloved mom, Betty Ruth Benson, a true believer in me and the good Lord. Praise and worship was our thing for a time and will be for a time yet to come.

Contents

Chapter One

···

Praise & Worship

he most boring of books starts now. Pauline sat down at her new, old-fashioned typewriter, black with silver keys and a lever to move the carriage. The typewriter was anything but secondhand; it only looked old. It was an electronic model, with a removable memory card. She started to type.

> The story begins in a time when faith was crucial. The world seemingly had changed without warning. The trumpets did sound, but what could anyone do about what was yet to come? Wasn't everything set in stone?

> No escape, the world was ceasing to exist as people knew it to be, especially those who lived within the United States. The hotel stays in Maui overlooking Flamingo Beach were all but a distant memory. States, cities and local establishments had

morphed into functional entries. People needed goods.

Was the intro too dramatic? Pauline, the author, was not sure, she continued. Her other book, *Faith Now*, was written with the same beginning. This book was to be the sequel to what she had written.

People needed safety, free of infection. A place where authority would be respected and rules would be enforced. And if possible, add a stopping point to mass hysteria which seemed to come and go randomly within certain locals. People needed a government that was not fractured. The enforcement of inherent individual rights as citizens would not be compromised by state and local governments. There was lots of moving parts, but nothing cohesive, no collective whole. At least those were Kara's thoughts, her main character.

Distracted, there was a nudge in the side of her stomach. Kara turned to see her sister open her piece of paper. It was a partial map with notes and pictures written on the side. "Really Kara, I could use your help. If you could spare some of your time that is.", said Naomi. She had a look to which Kara should have been accustomed.

The map was easy. Kara pointed to the building and then put her finger on a part of the map which was visible. She hugged her sister's arm and put her head on her shoulder as they continued to walk. Her mind soon returned to her friends at the beach and her former life. She longed to be together once more.

The GPS on most devices was no longer accurate so she and her sister had to make due. Terrorism was not only heightened but random. The prevention of the invasion of satellite-navigated UAV systems, unmanned ariel vehicles, made it almost impossible to get accurate coordinates in most destination. Armed drones by civilians were banned and spy cams were no longer allowed to be arial. Kara had kept in touch with Penny and Kelso through letters and sometimes phone calls if she could get a signal. So many things taken for granted were no longer accessible.

There was a mixture of old and new ways of doing things. At least that was Kara's understanding. When she and her sister met her friends, Penny and Kelso; it was many years ago at their favorite vacation spot in Maui. The two were whimsical and carefree entertaining the idea of marriage. They kept in touch over the years. Now their most current information regarding national state affairs came from her two friends. It was Kelso and Penny that kept her informed of what was becoming of the United States.

The old collegiate way of writing was tossed to the wayside. People could hardly remember the golden days of cameras with film, eight-tracks, the wired telephone, and the typewriter. *Now, it was cellular and cloudless, but the typewriter was at least still respected as a piece of equipment that embodied romanticism,* thought Pauline.

Pauline had purchased the iconic black typewriter to celebrate the first print of her last book, but it did not help her writing to go any faster. What was she going to write today? She had finished all of her morning activities: making her bed, brushing her teeth, taking out the trash, and cleaning the dishes. Now it was time for her to write something even more extraordinary than her last book. She put her hands together and stretched her fingers. The outline would be in her head.

Most times, her outline was beside her computer. This time there was only a blank piece of paper and pencil to jot down some of her thoughts from time to time, no constricting outline. Her computer was too much of a distraction for her. Her own thoughts were too much of a distraction for her; she laughed and yet, still nothing.

At any other time, the typewriter would be inviting. She eyed it as she rose in the morning and worked around it, smiling at the promise at what was yet to come. Writer's block or whatever it was that had her at a loss for words made her uncomfortable. It weighed her down like a load of lumber. She usually started her books with some attention-grabbing paragraph that not only drew the reader into her story but launched her into a writing frenzy. She continued where she left off on the state of future times for Kara and Naomi and the economy of the United States.

> Everything had changed to business as a priority although Maui was still beautiful. That was according to Kelso and Penny who were stationed at the hotel last time she communicated with them via text. The Carlton had

suffered financially from the lack of tourism but like many businesses they improvised. Being partially acquired by the government it not only functioned as a hostile but became a commerce center not just for the island and surrounding islands but for the nation and the world.

It was no longer an e-commerce environment but that of an old mercantile. Ships came from all over with their goods. The government had lowered all sanctions for Maui but still monitored everything that came into the island. The surrounding islands were fast becoming more fortified as a US military base.

This hotel in particular had become a highly secured area by the armed forces, which made it one of the safest places in the nation, especially its location as an island. There was almost no crime on that side of Maui or perhaps the whole island. Penny had texted that the island folk were like family and took care of each other without any regard for themselves. Kara wanted to go there again.

Sometimes the texts were longwinded and other times too short to properly understand. Kara would respond to some of Penny's text with a question mark. She made a mental picture of everything that Penny would say and eventually would write it down in one of her notebooks.

Other establishments and family abodes turned into Airbnb and offered room-and-board for essential government workers and such who were granted a temporary stay on the island to help with the current situation. Those who were in need of living quarters had commendations throughout the island. Although the island economy thrived it was no longer a tourist destination. It had evolved.

The typing stopped. Pauline was finished for the afternoon. If she could only come up with a title. Unfortunately, all that came to her mind was praise and worship—odd. Where did that come from? Who would ever read a story of praise and worship? But that was how the stories always started, with a whimsical thought. So she would persist. It was never wrong; somehow the story would evolve, and eventually it would be published, read, and sometimes even liked.

Praise … what was praise other than thanking God for everything that was given her? She was good at that. She thanked Him for the good and the bad, knowing He held both in the balance, being above, holy, 100 percent good with no shades of gray. Again, how boring was praise? But she knew it was a shortcut for not being depressed or agitated. If she praised God for the things that were most important, she found it hard to be distressed about her circumstances. It led to trust, but pooh, she had no intention of writing *Pilgrim's Progress*, or a shorter version, *The Christian's Secret of a Happy Life*, by Hannah Whitall Smith, explaining what it meant to praise and worship.

And what about worship? She couldn't force herself to worship, most of the time it came naturally. Should it be about how you feel? If she had to worship, she would listen to music, sing along, or worship at church. As it was, she usually was late to church and had avoided most of the worship songs altogether. That was until she heard a sermon on worship. It was about the part you do for God. It was the worship. She worshipped God in many ways, by acknowledging and praising Him and by making a joyful noise. As her Creator, humankind's Creator, and the Creator of the universe and beyond, He was worthy. "Okay, Lord. If this is from you, I'll be okay with it.", she said out loud. She put the title, Praise and Worship, at the beginning of the book. She wrote a little bit more on the infrastructure before there was a knock at the door.

> Food was dealt with differently. They were able to bring fish and game to one of the seven restaurants that had now been converted for the exchange of food and service. They could have something cooked and also have storage for their product frozen or for the future. The food was stored locally or on a neighboring island. It came with a percentage fee of an agreed-upon 15 percent of what they brought. It was highly encouraged that they should donate at least another 10 percent to those islanders in need, which was almost an assumed financial factor which was built into the exchange. The islanders loved to give.

> Local contributions made it possible for the hotel to make another building behind the local store which was within walking distance from the hotel. It served as a hub for goods and foods that had been discarded. It was accessible to anyone and steered the foot traffic away from the hotel facilities and onto the separate

property. As long as the local resident was designated as a point of contact for a family or business and cleared of any contagion, they were able to come and go and use the building as an exchange for used goods and commodities via the different venues.

Separate donations could be made. The donations consisted of everything. The things that no one wanted were shipped to the other parts of Hawaii and the United States. Kara kept track of all the details Penny texted and emailed.

Organizations for the different charities were many. Penny and Kelso headed up some of the islands' charity events in relation to the federal government; they were considered essential personnel while being housed at the hotel with their two children. They hoped to be able to stay on the island after the island was no longer commandeered. They loved the islands and those who lived there.

Many of the offshore shipments contained some of their nonessential goods, which were bought by outside vendors for a little over wholesale—a better deal than anywhere else in the United States. Companies made their money by reinventing themselves for a sub-economy that thrived on charity. The shops and restaurants that serviced the island as a whole did so as capitalists but kept moving forward, reinventing what everyone had accepted as convention.

Food stations and trucks became one of the modifications transporting leftover fresh produce and other food products. Kara had already decided that her and her sister would do just that. They could help with the meals and distribution of food if they were allowed to live on one of the islands. Kelso said he had connections, but everything was changing quickly.

Places of worship were the most essential part of the island. The churches were separated from the governmental facilities but were still federally protected. It was here that many people sought shelter who could not make it into the government housing. The sick, the elderly, the handicapped, the criminals, the mentally ill, the veterans, and anyone else who was not deemed essential or did not have their own funding or institution for protected and isolated housing were welcomed at places of worship.

The Christian church was the strongest establishment, and many of the pastors and veterans led the charge by way of leadership, worship, and organizational restructuring. It operated out of love and not fear. People were being healed and praising God. People were taking care of each other and watching out for one another. They had to band together to make things work.

The doctors and nurses within the converted hospitals, which now were assisted by the church, were giving better care to the veterans and those who had no healthcare at all. It was the same for education. The ratio of students to teachers, who were now specialized in their fields, was 20 to one.

Additional educational enhancements varied per county, but for most children Monday mornings started with the pledge of allegiance and a moment of prayer for God to keep America united and safe. "In God We Trust" was the banner over every institution, and all were welcome, no matter what religion they professed.

The community rallied around the churches. The hungry were fed, criminals were being visited, and families in general were not turned away. These were not only to whom help was offered but also were an essential part of ministries. Great donations came from the churches, which mostly were dropped off at the government centers for distribution. The church storehouse was also a local central repository for community staples.

The knock at the door woke her from thought. She quickly scribbled the words *praise and worship* on the page beside the typewriter and got up to answer to the door. As she walked toward the door, she noticed the dark skies from the dining room window. She could see the stranger from the side windows next to the front door.

The long paned windows were naked except

for streaks. She had tried to frost the windows, but it did not take. So she ended up having streaked them. Unfortunately, she could not remove the mess she had made. Some of her friends and neighbors had remarked that they liked what she had done. They mistook her for the do-it-yourself artist type, which she was not. She was the more practical type who just did not like people looking in her windows when she went to answer the door. She would buy narrow, thin curtains eventually but had not found the time to shop for them. She looked through the glass again. *Hmm*, she thought. In the doorway stood a tall and lanky male, with long pulled-back hair, dressed in dark drab colors.

She pressed her intercom button. It was an old feature of the home that she found came in handy. "Can I help you?" said Pauline. He pounded on the door with his fist. As the thumps grew louder, she lifted her phone to call nine-one-one.

The windows on both sides of the front door would be little protection if he decided to break the glass to find his way through and open the door. It was still daytime, although the shaded sky robbed the sun of its light. It seemed an unlikely time for a random theft.

"Lady! Open the door! I need help, *now*," said the man. She wasn't sure if she had seen blood or not, but she instinctively responded and opened the door. He stumbled into the house.

She could see him clearly now. His head was bandaged, and his eyes could not focus. There was no blood, but definitely he was on something. Praise and worship came back into her head. *You have got to be kidding me, God, for real?* She thought to herself. "What can I do?" she asked. "Do you need my phone to make a phone call?" She pulled out a dining room chair.

Charlie took a seat and looked up at her as best he could. He shook his head. *For real,* he thought. *Are you so stupid you would let a stranger into your home without any security and hand me your phone? Where's your dog?* He knew she did not have a dog. He had watched her house for a couple of weeks. He was aware of what she did for a living and who was her closest friend—nobody. He knew her daily routine and that she basically had no life other than church, casual friends, and family. *She was a stick-in-the-mud and ugly, too,* he thought. But would he take her life for a trophy and some trinkets? Modest tastes, she had little. He could think of no one more pathetic in his life than this woman. "Water, can I have a glass of water?" he said in a raspy voice.

Pauline had already texted her next-door neighbor to come visit. The text that was sent from the stranger's phone was simple. *Not yet,* he texted. She watched him with his phone. Nothing about this felt right. She began to hum, "Be Thou My Vision."

She checked her phone; nothing yet. She started to eye the exits in her home. She was too panicked to talk to God, yet she hummed on, now louder. She returned to the table with a glass of water.

Another knock on her door, and her heart raced. The man turned to see who it was, as if he was expecting someone. She recognized the body shape through the window. It was her neighbor. She waved to the stranger to stay seated.

The door opened before she reached the intercom. She hugged him, overjoyed. "Hah, Bert, I must have forgot to lock the door. What a pleasantry this is.", she said. She was trying to sound normal, but nobody ever spoke like that. She wanted to say it was unexpected, but it was not, as she had already texted him, *Hurry.*

The man looked at his phone. A text appeared, *Hangin' back.* He lifted himself from the chair as if he was hurt and went to shake the neighbor's hand. *This is unexpected*, thought the stranger, *not good.*

The word *pleasantry* hung in the air. Bert was in law enforcement. He made a living from picking up clues, like odd phrases that smelled of desperation. He made a sharp assessment of the man. *Trouble* was his only noun. He did not want to shake anyone's hand—not because he had a haughty disposition, but because he had been digging in the soil. He hoped to have his begonias planted before the storm. He extended his dirty hand anyway and held the man's hand a little too long. "So what brings you this way? Pauline said you were having trouble, car?" said Bert.

The man looked at Pauline with surprise. *Smart of her to text that*, the man thought. But Pauline had not texted anything about car trouble, only to come over. Bert presumed the rest. He did not want the man to think Pauline was scared, thus her reason for texting him, or that she was easy prey. Something was up; he just did not know what it was yet.

Thunder rolled and then there was a flash of light. The stranger's gaze became steady as he leaned into Bert like he was going to tell him a secret or as if he was inebriated. The man had made his own assumption and smelled cop. Not just a cop, but someone of strength, who was discerning. "No, just scared, a friend of mine was jealous of me and his woman. I just got out of the hospital. That is how I got the head injury. He said he was going to bash my head in again. I was in a car accident, bro. He tried to run me over.", said the man. Pauline and Bert exchanged looks. "Thanks for letting me in when you did. I could be dead. They're looking for me," said the man.

The story was plausible. It was even partly true. The head injury was from an accident where someone had tried to run him over with a car. His cousin, Verna, who was a nurse, bandaged his head and prescribed him some painkillers. It was why his eyes could not focus. He was doped up.

Car lights shined through the dining room windows.

The stranger thought it might be someone from his group doing something asinine. Bert opened the front door and waved to one of his neighbors. "It's one of our neighbors," he said to Pauline. The stranger was relieved. "So how'd you get here, and do you need me to take you somewhere?" he asked.

The stranger shook his head, making it throb. The narrative stuck, and he knew it. "No, you a cop, yeah? Can't tell you anything. You know how it is.", said the man. He was smarter than most; he wasn't packing and hadn't broken any laws. Everyone got in trouble trying to be something they were not—good. They gave out too much information, trying to snow the cops into believing better. He was just himself, not good, not bad, just somewhere in between.

His mother always told him he was too honest for his own well-being. She had brought him up to hate cops. The only thing he respected was the back of her hand, which, as he grew older, was no longer effective. He became obedient, but only to himself.

The door was open again. Bert took a bow as he extended his arm toward the door. The man smiled a wiry smile. Pauline did something unexpected. She not only smiled back but took his hand. He tried to grab it back, but her grip was firmer than he expected. He had felt that hand before in his life. There it was, in her words. "Drugs are the devil's highway to your heart," she said prophesying of the potential danger. It was his grandmother. She had made him promise even at a young age that he would guard his heart from evil, pray, and stay away from drugs.

He paused and looked at Pauline as if she was the devil and pulled his hand back. His grandmother's words gripped him firmly. Those words called him back into a time that was erased from his memory. She sang songs of Jesus and "Be Thou My Vision." It was Grandma and Grandpa who had raised him. They never lifted a hand to him, except to swat him on the butt as a toddler, but they were firm with him. He was eight years old when his mother came and got him. It was life that was good, but he had forgotten, and it had forgotten him.

The doorway widened as Bert extended his arm even further out. "Charlie, my name is Charlie," the stranger said. "Don't pray for me, got it!" He was now totally sober and terrified. They watched as he vanished down the street, walking but almost running. He looked back at the house with so much pain in his eyes that Pauline teared up and prayed, although she was not sure what had just happened. She only knew that somebody had been praying for that young man, and Jesus loved him.

The door shut, and Bert shook his head. "I don't want to hear it. I already know," said Pauline. "I messed up." She walked into the kitchen through the dining room. Bert followed.

The sink faced the kitchen table and the sunroom. She stopped at the sink and pulled out the faucet. He then took the handle and sprayed his hands and arms. She took the liberty of dabbing the soap onto his hands and arms for him. "It is just that I can't always be home when you welcome in strangers", said Bert. "Pauline, you have to understand. It's not safe for you to be so welcoming." He washed his hands and arms, and Pauline handed him a dish towel.

The storm had moved closer. Lightning flashed as it thundered again and was heard in the distance. "I am fine. If I didn't text you, I would have called or texted"—she paused. There was no other option than Bert who lived nearby. "Someone else, I could have dialed nine-one-one. Besides, this area is relatively safe."

They watched as the rain streamed down the sunroom windows. She pulled out some lasagna left over from the night before and plated two pieces. "Nothing like leftovers, but the lasagna is at least homemade. How can anyone ever tire of lasagna?" said Pauline, hoping to change the subject. She held up a bottle of wine, but he shook his head no, so she retrieved the pitcher of half lemonade and tea from the refrigerator and a salad.

The pitcher was placed on the counter. "I made my own version of half tea and lemonade, too." Bert looked confused. "Instead of buying cans I made my own version of half tea and lemonade." She placed the plates and salad on the table.

The silverware and the napkins were already in Bert's hand as he continued to lecture her. He hated talking to Pauline like she was a child, but could not stop himself. "You have that serendipitous lifestyle that lends itself to stupidity. You live by yourself, without even a goldfish. You need to be more cautious."

She tilted her head in disbelief. Her small frame came against Bert's robust body. "You had your chance to tell me what to do. We tried this, and it did not work out for either of us," she said. She opened the cabinet and reached for the tumblers and filled them with the half and half tea. "I don't appreciate you talking to me as a child. I am just fine by myself. I don't need a security system or goldfish. I have my typewriter," she said and thought about Charlie. "I don't normally let strangers into my home. Charlie needed a place to be, nothing so unsettling about that. Maybe it was a bad decision to welcome him, but it was impulse. He sounded desperate," she said, replaying it in her head. "I concede, it was a bad decision."

The more Bert thought about her words, the madder he became. He was not sure he wanted to stay to eat with her. "That's right, it did not work," he said. He was no longer focused on Charlie. "It was not the both of us, it was you. You just wanted to be with you. That's what you said. How does that have anything to do with me?" said Bert. She was vexing and mulish which overpowered even her most attractive physical attributes.

21

The white candle was lit and was carried to the table almost as a surrender. As Bert set it down he smiled at Pauline and wondered why he was not better off without her. "Humm," she said. "Well, the point is there is not an us, just a you and me, and me thanks you for coming to my rescue." She cheerfully carried the typewriter and notes from the table to the cabinet before sitting down across from Bert.

Bert grabbed her hand. They bowed their heads and prayed. She was grateful. She had not seen him in over three months, and to the best of her knowledge he had not moved on to any other relationship. After all, he was there with her on a Sunday night. She would ask later just to make sure. They ate and talked about old times. She only wished she had been a better friend to him while they were dating. She was all about herself, and she knew it.

After dinner they adjourned to the sunroom to play cards. Bert no longer cared that he did not get his begonias planted. He was glad to have been there for Pauline when she needed him. As for Charlie, he had one of those faces. Bert could not help but think he had seen Charlie somewhere before, his mug shot, either in the books or in person at the station, or maybe it had been an arrest. He also had a feeling it would not be the last they would see of him. As Bert walked home that night, he felt a renewed sense of hope. He decided he needed to try a little harder to win over Pauline.

Chapter Two

What's Next?

The next morning was a good morning. The sun shined through the window patting her with its light and telling her it was time for her to get up and not roll over, but like the unproductive person she was, she rolled over one last time putting an extra pillow in front of her face to block its light. It lasted about ten minutes before she lowered her legs on the side of her bed and then shuffled her feet across the wooden floor to the bathroom.

The day's itinerary was anything but full. She showered, dressed and figured she could take it easy and maybe have a half a day of writing. She'd had all night to think about her story line, which once again was sparse beyond praise and worship—two words that would work their way into her life and thinking, but she was not sure that she wouldn't tire of them.

The coffee was already brewed by the time she walked downstairs. She opened the door to collect her local newspaper which had neatly been placed inside a basket which contained a small begonia plant. She did not have to guess from whom it came. She looked both ways but there was no-one in sight. Bert had probably left it much earlier on his way to the station. She would pray for him, as she constantly was hearing how dangerous it was for police officers out in the field. They no longer aired cop shows on television because it was becoming too easy to target certain cops. The world was changing rapidly.

There it was an inspiration. She started to write. The thoughts came quickly as she anticipated what the future now looked like for Kara and her sister Naomi. She finished writing about the church and the different functions on the islands so how was it different for Naomi and Kara? They did not live such a carefree lifestyle in their neck of the woods.

> It was a cold brisk morning when Kara decided to take one of her infamous long walks to clear her head. She had only gone a couple miles before she no longer recognized where she was and had no signal.

> Not only had she gone in the wrong direction, but she had no idea what the right direction was. She could picture Naomi waiting for her with her arms crossed. *Oh, Naomi, if only you had come with me. We would be lost together.* Kara

giggled at the thought of how annoyed she would be.

The sim card was popped out of the phone and back into it. She reset the network settings and once again she had a single bar signal. She quickly sent her location to her sister. Sadly, the assumption could be made that she also was off the grid.

The signal was gone. She should have called the local authorities although they no longer assisted in disseminating information. What was left of the police force was deputized vigilantes, to which they did not subscribe. The flavor was whatever the state or community would allow with few rules that protected their individual rights, especially innocent until proven guilty. It was the freedom of being treated innocent before being convicted that she and her sister would never give up, even if it cost them their lives.

People were numbered. They were given a number under control of a more sovereign citizenship to keep track of individuals. It fell under no authority and no real accountability, which in itself was the devil, Kara thought. Anyway, it would not be of any help to Kara since she still refused to get the number. Unfortunately, she could not be tracked if she disappeared. Even if being numbered helped with obtaining food and supplies it was not worth it for the both of them. And although Naomi did not believe in the devil, she would not take the mark. She said it was evil, too.

God's authority is greater. What does that look like? Kara believed in the devil but wasn't sure what the devil would look like either—whether it just had horns or blue jeans. The knowledge of what was evil versus what was good was the deciding factor for authority. The look of good was creation itself. The authority of a sovereign God had to be greater if it were to encompass evil or all would be good but tainted which is no good. There had to be a plan for both.

Both was to be seen. Kara could see both and the evil could not come from the same place as the good. She knew the devil existed and it was associated with a different type of citizenship, one of numbers. Similarly, she started to see creation as a whole, and the divinity that surrounded His children. They had no number except the number of the hairs on their head for which God Himself accounted.

It was a kingdom divided. There was no ultimate sovereignty. Everyone pointed fingers at everyone else even within the same family. They were divided; at first it seemed over politics, but then it went deeper. As certain events unfolded people became more and more discontent.

It was a minute. Kara turned around to take the best direction she knew to make her way home. Finally she saw someone familiar. It was Naomi. She wasn't mad, but they did not talk for the first mile back home. "Naomi, did you see my location?", asked Kara. Naomi shook her head no.

The tree branches bent over them. "We need to be home before our local curfew, so don't talk, just walk.", said Naomi. "It was not hard to track you. You start off in the same direction and overtime you just go further and further into the woods. I just followed your original path and waited.", she said and smiled. "I guess you found me."

★★★

The small influx of words were not enough. The King James Bible sat on the shelf by the fireplace in the downstairs family room. Pauline went to retrieve it. Quiet time was not a daily occurrence, but she figured if nothing was coming to her, she probably needed to go to the a good source for inspiration. Pauline found that time spent in the Bible and prayer always helped her mind and heart to be right from that point. She did not read on the topic of worship or praise; she just continued where she had left off in the Bible. Today it was the book of Mark. She habitually read through the Bible with no deadline. It kept her connected, like it was her own secret garden where she would go and meet with God.

After spending some time in the Word, she once again sat before her typewriter, still ecstatic about her newly purchased gadget. She placed her piece of paper beside it and thought about what to type. The setting of the story would be a futuristic day when people no longer acknowledged God as the creator. The strain of religious people had to hide their worship. It would be similar to what occurs in some countries today which do not have same religious freedoms and protection of religion as in the USA. Pauline started to type.

> There was no pleasure in the normal tasks of the day, an oppression that created depression among even the most positive of positive people. The skies were dark. Music was not played. People were afraid to go outside, and yet inside Kara's heart was Hope. She did not know of her God as her Jewish ancestors had, but still believed. *What a glorious God,* she thought, *if any of it was true, a special people that were set apart for Him, that were directed and protected by Him.*

The typewriter stopped clicking. She looked at her phone to see the text. *Is now a good time?* It was from a relative for whom she barely cared. Before she could answer the text came the call. "Hey, Sam, what's up?" asked Pauline. There was no answer. Sam was busy typing a message. "Sam?" she repeated.

The phone call was now on speaker. "Yes, Samantha here. No, I did not, but I'll have it to you." She paused and started typing. "By tomorrow morning. Good?" Pauline was not good or happy as she waited for Sam to finish her teleconferencing on her computer.

She placed her phone on the table next to her piece of paper and hit speaker. *Two can play at that game*, she thought to herself. "Sam, let me let you go. You can call me later when you have more time, and you're not busy."

Sammie now took her phone off of speaker and placed it next to her ear. "No, Pauline, wait. I know you're busy too, still writing? Don't answer, you can tell me about it some other time. More importantly, it is about my wedding. Is it okay if—?" She paused again and started typing. This time it was a long pause.

Pauline waited and hoped she was not going to ask her to be in her wedding party. She had forgotten that Sam was even getting married. "Is it okay if we invite you to the wedding but not to the reception? I am sending out my 'save the date' with an RSVP attached." said Sam. "You don't have to get us a gift, but you should, etiquette. I just definitely want you there to bless our marriage, but sadly we've overextended ourselves on our reception invites. We are up to 125 people, and we really need to be at 120 attendees. My fiancé is being rather firm on that number. That is how they are at times, a fiancé that is." said Sammie. Again the typing started.

It was not funny. Pauline took most things pretty seriously, and this was no exception. "Sammie, are you kidding me? No, it's not okay. Half the people who respond are not going to be able to make it. Call me after everyone has responded to your RSVP, and then ask me. I expect my invite in the mail this week, and I want a plus-one.", said Pauline. She now was starting to have a sense of humor about it.

Sam looked at her phone and made a face and took it off speaker. "A plus-one, are you sure? Who would you bring?" she asked. "Oh, you have a boyfriend? Oh, oh, okay, that's fine. I am not even doing invites right now, just 'save the date' with an RSVP." It was quiet on both ends of the line.

Pauline envisioned Sam with her neck tilted as she tried to balance her smartphone between her head and her neck as she typed, but her typing again stopped as she waited for Pauline's answer. "No, I don't have a boyfriend," said Pauline. "Okay, I still want mine with a plus-one option when you do send it out. I am going to go now. Take care, cousin." The line went dead. She was trying to remain nice but hoped Sam would get a crick in her neck that was not so easily remedied by aspirin. Her story began again with Kara and Naomi trying to make the best of the shortage for food and supplies.

★★★

What is the purpose of life if everyone lived less than a century? Kara lifted a dented can for her sister to see. Naomi shrugged her shoulders so Kara put it in her backpack. Eternity was far fetched, but her own life was too short for its purpose to be tied up in one generation only. Kara pondered everything. Her reflective reasoning was sometimes circular, which maddened those around her. She was no longer hungry as she and her sister ate as they pillaged food from the family's home next door. They made their way back to their condo.

The condo that they stayed in was a decent shelter. There was not a lot of light, though the candles were lit. They did not want to be seen from the road. The looters had come and gone and had taken what they wanted. Friends of their parents that lived next door had left with their house armed several months ago. They gave the girls the code. It was like Fort Knox, but as long as you had the code or codes, you were able to get into anything. So while most people had nothing, Kara and her sister had access to much.

They sat quietly next to each other reading. Kara was reading works from a Jewish writer. It started out with a woman who had smuggled a baby home during a time of persecution and war.

The faith based book was worn as the pages that Kara turned were ear marked. "Don't you think you have anything better to think about then theology?" asked Kara's sister Naomi, older by six years and taller by six inches. "'What happened?' is a better question than the things you ask: 'Why? Is there a purpose?' Stop with those questions. We are survivors. If we ever get to be vacationing again in Maui or if we ever get to a safe-haven like that, then we can think lofty things. We can have superior philosophical and theological thoughts and conversations over a latte or chai beverage of choice."

Kara snickered. Naomi always knew how to make her laugh, whether it was intentional or not.

★★★

Charlie made it back to his den the next day with time to spare. He had given Lucille, another member of the group, additional information on the neighborhood, the night before in a text. They also had their own responsibilities for any heist. Nothing to add for his contribution, other than a pale, pasty complexion that was disconcerting for the other three people in the room, Charlie stood in the doorway.

In a smoke filled room, Stern stumbled a few feet mocking Charlie. He was first to approach Charlie. He was the sectarian of the group, very dogmatic about how he thought things should be done, thinking through everything. If someone else did not step up to bat, the alpha would become his role, even though he'd been the last member to join the group.

Usually, Stern would bite his tongue and go along with the flow waiting for the time when he would convince everyone that he was the true leader. This time was one of those times he seized the moment. There was blood in the water and he circled.

All eyes were on Stern as he paced the room and then found his way back to the easy chair and sprawled himself across it sideways. "So, Charlie," he said, sensing something had gone wrong. "What did you find out? Is she still on the docket for a little bit of fun and meanness?" Stern was looking for answers and a reaction.

Sweat poured across Charlie's face. He knew they were looking for a reaction, but what they were seeing was a mixture of a headache, alcohol, and painkillers, so he went with it. He stumbled around the room like a drunk person, playing the part.

The pills were on the kitchen table where had he left them, and he was heading that way. Charlie was the undesignated leader of the group and had not been crossed up until now. He already knew, like a lightning bolt to a tree, he was hit and divided, he could not go back to that home. Pauline could no longer be their mark.

Everything was slowly coming back into focus. He was not the same person he was a week ago or even yesterday, but he was not letting go. He looked at Stern, who may have been more evil but not more intelligent, and decided quickly not to challenge him as he saw two of him and figured he could not be that unlucky. "Hey, not now. Let me take my pills first, then we can figure where we are," he said. "Let Lucille tell us about the cop on the street."

It was a handoff and played well. Stern stood up and poured himself a glass of water. A cop, how could that be? How could he have missed it? Everyone was supposed to be out of the neighborhood, and there were no cops. "Bert is a friend of hers and doesn't come by on a regular basis," said Lucille, but she only knew what Charlie had texted.

35

The text was simple. It was for her eyes only and to be deleted. The message showed a face with eyes closed and xxx. She had coded messages that she only shared with Charlie. Sometimes, the eyes with xxx meant that he or she had seen or done something that could not be undone. They had gotten pretty good at conversations with only codes. His message was easy. Charlie never gave kisses, so the xxx meant to delete or that something went wrong. The eyes closed could be sleep or that no one else could see the message. Instead of what appeared to be Charlie wishing her a good night's sleep with kisses and closed eyes, she had guessed right.

Lucille wondered why Charlie would have cared to let her off the hook; it was her job to know that the cop lived on the street and was a friend of Pauline's. He had no reason to help her out other than he would look bad as the leader of the group if everything did not go smoothly. Unlikely, though, he had something else up his sleeve. She figured she should have been in trouble with him. Stern was in charge of backing up the information. He would double-check the sources. Bingo, she thought, he wanted it to be Stern's fault. It was a rooster fight.

The weight was lifted. Lucille was glad it was not on her. Her punishment would have been something that involved money, like part of her share of whatever was going down. She really did not care about money the way other people did, but she still did not like giving up her stuff. She looked at Charlie; something had changed in him. She sensed weakness and was frightened for the outcome. She pondered it but not for long; he was still Charlie.

The teen years and more innocent lives, for the both of them, transitioned swiftly. She had known him for too long. He was only for himself for as long as she had known him, but at one time they were innocent. It was the ombre shadow darkness that always followed the both of them. They drew strength from it. It was not the complete utter darkness but rather the shades of light in which they bonded, but neither of them knew what to do with the light.

The darkness would lift, at least partially, and hope would enter. Lucille could feel it was one of those times. Both she and Charlie would notice it at the same time.

It was if there was a heaviness in the air that would not leave; then somehow things would be positive again. There were certain things that they knew to stay away from like heavy drugs, dealing, or using. It definitely brought an air of oppression, but this was different than that. This was separate.

There was a darkness coming; she could feel it in her bones, but maybe she was just going crazy. She mentioned it to Charlie, but he told her not to talk about it. He was not interesting in hearing her viewpoints unless she was willing to pay him to listen. The first time he said it, it was funny. After that she realized he meant it. It got to the point where he would hold out his hand if she said anything personal. Their private conversations were few and far between; nearly all their talks had to do with a job. The job, no matter what it was, always came first.

Stern came close to Lucille. She could feel his negative energy and smell his breath behind her. She stiffened but would not move. She would stand up to him even if she would lose the fight. He put his hand on the back of her shirt and slowly went up to the nape of her neck. She could feel his grip tighten and she shuddered. "Good intel, Lucy, dear," said Stern, "Think we could have known it a little sooner than now?" He looked at her neck as her redeeming feature.

There would be no rescue for her. She knew that, had any one of them decided to turn on her, she could defend herself, but she could not be the one to draw fatal blood. She pretended not to have a conscience, but she did. She'd been raised with discipline and respect. No one meant anything to her, but she still did not want them dead. She knew she needed to leave the group but had no idea how to make that exit. Nor did she know why she stayed, except maybe it was Charlie, some sort of loyalty, she guessed.

Charlie grabbed Stern's glass of water and filled it up. The double vision was still there, but he had seen worse. He gulped the water and slammed the glass down on the counter, breaking it in pieces and taking the largest piece into his palm. Treble, the only true follower in the group, followed Charlie's command as he pointed to the glass on the table.

Stern turned around to see the broken glass, which Treble had already started to pick up. "I'm better now. Sorry about your glass of water. Had to have my pills," said Charlie as he avoided the shards of glass and walked over to Lucille. "Hey, it was a dry run, no hard feelings."

The glass had a sharp edge that Charlie kept next to his shirtsleeve. "Lucille told me," he said, "but you told me there was none in the neighborhood who would be accessible for Pauline to reach if we had her phone. Yet Bert, the cop, was at her front door within a minute." He went to pat Stern on back, and with the other hand he pushed the piece of glass against his neck. "The moral of the story is that we need you to do your job, but like I said, this was just a dry run."

Charlie took away the piece of glass. Stern took the threat with a grain of salt, next time he would have the advantage and it would be someone else's neck. Charlie had just become leader, and Stern would fall in line for a time.

Treble asked if it was okay if he started the vacuum. Lucille said it would be fine and exchanged looks with Charlie. It was their secret, and he had her back. Now she knew. Charlie was beaten up from his accident, painkillers, and alcohol but still handled himself well. She regained her faith in Charlie, but still felt like he had changed somehow.

"Hey, Treble, what do you think about us doing a scouting trip?" said Charlie. "We'll see whereabouts this dude lives and what kind of character he is. He can't be too tough of a cop." Treble agreed.

The kitchen was right off of the living room in a small ranch house that Charlie had bought for next to nothing. It was a house where dealers sold drugs. It needed a total gut job, and every room needed major renovations, but Charlie didn't care; he didn't sleep there. The cops left it alone. There was no one coming to and from the house any longer to buy and sell drugs. It was only the band of four: Treble, Lucille, Charlie and now Stern. The police, understaffed anyway, had no reason to bother.

Chapter Three

Detective

*A*nother day, another dollar. Bert tried to act like the day was normal, but it was anything but common. Everyday things got a little worse. The corruption within the precinct only correlated with the lack of funding and declining respect for authority. He wished things were different or he could be the change, but he did not know where to start. He was one of the only officers left who hit the beat and yet did not have connections on the other side. It was not always obvious, but the dishonest dealings were there. It was said things ran more smoothly and criminals still got arrested, but somehow he only knew the straight and narrow. He called it as he saw it. If you did wrong, it wasn't right, no matter whether you were on the side of defending the law or receiving it.

Most of his coworkers agreed that it was not that simple. His partner and best friend on the force, Jay, said something distinct: not being loved comes at a price. He knew more than the others and was right. Neither side loved or liked him, and it was obvious.

The job was becoming increasingly hard. They watched for him on the streets as well as in the office. He was good at finding criminal activity. He had turned down the promotion to captain and a request to become a detective because he chose to work the streets instead. It was there that he did the most good. It was tiresome arresting people for the same crimes over and over again relentlessly, but that was his job, and he did it too well.

Jay also held to the code of honor but was ready for a change. He had requested a transfer to a better part of the state with higher-rated schools and less crime. He would move his family to a safer district, a little further out. It was also would be less expensive. He said they had a target on their backs for which both sides aimed. It was true, but Bert thought if his days were numbered, he would do right by them.

It had been a long day. Jay and Bert made five arrests, all of them drug-related, with other charges tacked on having to do with firearms, a DWI, and a theft. "If only people could kick their habits," Jay said as he lit a cigarette in front of the station. Bert shook his head, looking down at the ground. He was glad the day had come to a close. They had walked out together, but Jay had to double back to talk with Captain Jaks after he received a text. Bert turned around to go with him. "No, I'm sure it has to do with my transfer. You have a good night," said Jay and waved.

The garage was across the street hidden behind some shops and a pizza parlor. Bert crossed the street and turned around to see that Jay was no longer there. He was more sentimental than most. The department would replace Jay with a new partner, but he would not be of the same caliber. Bert was alone, and it would stay that way, the lone warrior for good. He shook his head sadly. He unlocked his truck and started his drive homeward.

The traffic light turned green. Bert was on the phone with Sara, a coworker. She was one of the many people working at the station who thought Bert was the "bee's knees," as she would put it. She found him interesting and charming and wouldn't quit. "If you could be there, I would make your favorite dessert." Sara paused and waited for him to respond. "It would only be for a couple of hours. It's a small group of people." He began to ask her how she knew what his favorite dessert was, knowing he did not have one. The light turned green, and he started to pull forward.

The intersection was clear until the utility truck sped through the red light, crashing into Bert's truck. The utility truck was in the left lane turning left, but instead of turning left, the driver jolted the truck out of its lane and gassed it. It came in a straight line and headed right for the driver's side of his truck.

Bert slammed on his brakes as he was still going slow, and the truck slid past him, hitting his front bumper and spinning the truck horizontally and then the opposite direction. All the while, as the driver passed him, he was giving him the middle finger. The car behind him followed out in the intersection and barely touched Bert's front bumper.

Sara heard the crash and asked if he was all right. "Sara, I have to go. I just got into a car accident," said Bert. "Wait, Sara, are you still at work?"

She did not answer directly but just asked, "What are we dispatching?" The surroundings should have been blurred, but he was able to be blurt out every detail of the hit-and-run, down to the color of shirt the man was wearing and the company of the utility truck.

He heard the sirens before she had even finished putting in the order. The squad cars raced past his truck while a squad car coming from behind stopped in the middle of the intersection. The driver of the car that had hit him was a woman that he knew from church. Her name was Jan. She rushed out of her to his truck to see if he was okay. She was surprised to see it was Bert. "Oh, Bert, I didn't know it was you. Are you okay? I saw everything. He ran a red light and didn't stop."

Still a little out of it, he surveyed his surroundings. He felt the back of his neck. "Yeah, I'm fine. How are you?" he asked. One of the cops had already stopped the traffic light and was directing traffic.

Jan handed Bert a card. "Okay, it was barely a bump of my bumper to your bumper, from one bumper to the other … it was just a bump.", she said. She smiled sweetly. Bert turned his head slightly and rolled his eyes. He laughed and her laughter followed.

It would hurt more later. He rubbed the back of his neck again. "I'm not worried. Are you sure you are okay?", asked Bert. She nodded. "Then no worries, I'll see you at church on Sunday", said Bert. She put her hand on his forearm. She could feel his strength and was embarrassed but even so she still kept her hand on his arm. "Give your statement to the other officer.", said Bert.

She studied his features and the outline of his face. It was rugged with a strong jawline, every facial wrinkle adding more character. This is closer than she had ever gotten to him at church and she liked it. "Here's my information in case there is any damage. She squeezed his arm as it hung out of his window. "I would love to get together sometime for anything if you have the time, anytime." she said with another smile. *There it was again.* He laughed once more at the awkward phrasing. This time she was not sure why he laughed other than he wasn't interested.

Jan was quiet. She walked away and hoped she had not made things awkward. She planned on giving her realtor business card with her insurance information to whomever she bumped, but she was glad it was Bert. She felt like she was being opportunistic, but she did not care.

Women can be trouble. Bert on the other hand was caught off-guard. The younger him would have yelled after her, 'I'll find the time.', but the older him did not need to complicate things. He needed to stere clear of stumbling blocks. Right now, he was okay.

The night just became longer. As if he was not already unhappy, now he had to look forward to things being awkward at church. He tried not to feel sorry for himself, but it seemed like his life was just not great. He kept himself from thinking negative thoughts, but there were too many of them for some not to slip through into his consciousness. So he fixed himself on counting his blessings: his relationship with the Lord, a great home, a decent truck (although now it was damaged), his sexy neighbor, some friends, family, a good church, and food. It left off there as he finally started for home.

The damage to the truck was minimal. He drove it home and pulled into his driveway slowly. He heard a new rattling for which he could not account. As for the rest of the truck, the front and left side were bent, but he would have them fixed quickly. He would not have the truck totaled even if the frame was damaged. It was one of his prized possessions.

The house appeared dark and dreary. The house and driveway lights did not turn on at the proper time. He had forgot to reset his light automation schedule for the fall or put it on sensor. He made a mental note to do so. He parked his truck in the driveway as he did sometimes when he was working on something in the garage. His latest project was cabinets.

He walked down the driveway, opened his mailbox, and pulled out a small package and some letters. He read them as he walked up his front steps. As he pulled opened the screen door, a thank you note dropped down by his foot. He picked it up and unlocked the door. The house had an odd odor to it; he was sure it was nothing, but it smelled like wet dog. The whiff got stronger toward the kitchen.

There was nothing out of the ordinary. The trash bin had been emptied. He went to the back door, which was slid open; the screen door was shut and locked. The smell intensified as he walked outside. He stood on the deck, where the scent of an animal overpowered him. He quickly found a small buck dead on the ground. He studied it for a few seconds. The rack, unfortunately, was not worth mentioning. The buck had been shot. He assumed the deer had meandered into his backyard wounded and fallen down dead.

Once a hunter, it is hard to give it up. There is always a need; otherwise the ecosystem suffers. Bert was an only child and had grown up with his grandparents and his father, not far from where he lived now. He loved hunting with his granddad and pops. His two favorite pastimes growing up were hunting and fishing; any chance he had, he was doing one of the two. His father was sheriff but died in the line of duty. Some of his best memories were hunting.

It was not an uncommon occurrence that a deer shot, if not killed immediately, would outrun its hunter. It had not been dead and in his backyard for long. He guesstimated less than twenty-four hours, but long enough for the scent of deer to penetrate his home. Burt took out his pistol and shot it in the head.

There was a little rustling in the woods, but Bert could see nothing. Seasonal hunting was a pastime that was legal in his parts of the woods as long as you knew what you were hunting, had a gaming license, and were not hunting on private property without permission. His own property backed some public and private acreage, so it was hard to say where the deer had come from. He surveyed his surroundings and listened for shots but saw and heard nothing.

The yard had been nicely landscaped. There was a brick firepit and wooden benches not far from the house. In a nearby corner of the property there was a huge koi pond and water feature which added the soothing effect of a waterfall. He had thought about saving up for a pool but decided that in his old age it would be a retirement present to himself—when his knees were destroyed and he could no longer go for a long run or hike. It would mostly be used for exercise, but he expected it to add a certain "je ne sais quoi" that his large yard needed.

The pairs of binoculars were fitted with night vision. Two camouflaged men stood quietly behind their binoculars. What Bert did not see in the night they could see perfectly, but their focus was only on one man. Their prey and sport was not animal but human. They had stuck around to observe his habits. They were apprised of his accident, so they hunkered down for a long night, waiting. They needed to see how he rolled so that when they took him out, it could not be traced back to anyone who knew him, but he was a wanted man and everyone knew it. They reported everything they saw back to their employer so that they could plan for Bert's demise.

None the wiser, Bert had not been hunting in a minute, but had he known he was being hunted, he would know just what to look for: tracks. It was a good night. After all, the Lord had seen fit, after the day he'd had, to put a future dinner on his doorstep. He rolled up his sleeves; his work was just beginning. He would need to cut and hang the deer for a couple of days. He was lucky the temperature outside was just right for him to do so. The whole process, aside from rigging something up, would take him a couple of hours.

The concrete pavement under the deck was perfect for this type of work. It had shade and was out of the way.

Once prepped, the deer could hang outside his ten-by-ten storage room for the next two days without anyone noticing. That is, unless they went downstairs to his family room, which opened into the backyard; then the deer would be front and center.

The downstairs had easy access to where he would be working. The more Bert thought about it, the more excited he became. The deer could be hung where it would not be seen unless you were behind the house. It would be near his motion sensor camera so he could keep an eye on it remotely if necessary. It would be outside his house so the smell would be minimal from the inside. He could not wait to start work.

The coffee cups hung on a rack on the wall. He eyed them, pondering which one to choose. Although he was not supposed to have coffee at night, he had work to do. He would be better suited for a brandy, but tonight he chose caffeine. He tried not to make alcohol a habit. Too easy to unwind; he liked to be on his toes, no impaired judgment. Nothing wrong for the normal folks but he was called to be sober.

The temptation came and went. Tomorrow would bring a headache either way. He rubbed his neck and the base of his skull. It was probably a pinched nerve. Red wine might be the ticket to thin out his blood, but again he opened the cabinet next to the fridge and chose an alternative, aspirin.

The red coffeemaker was at the end of the counter. The coffee mugs on display had been collected over a lifetime. He chose "Keep America Great," and on the other side of the ceramic mug was "Trust In God." The coffee machine worked by command. "Alexa," Bert said in a master's tone, "brew." After the brewing started came one more command to Alexa. "Play my classical music station by Pandora." She agreed as she always did and repeated the request to make sure she got it right.

The deer had appeared by luck. They watched as the fatally shot deer stumbled a hundred yards away. The two men chased and prodded the buck into Bert's backyard. It was as if it sought out help, but found none, stumbling to its death a few yards from the house. The foreshadowing and irony of events for Belmont, an assumed name, was not lost. The buck was destined for death and found its way to Bert's house. Across the few feet between them, he told his partner, Derby, also an assumed name, that it was a sign.

Derby twisted his head to study his friend. "How can you be so great at what you do and so dismally dumb?" Derby was not attached to anyone, especially not Belmont, and was not humble enough to think anyone could take him or compete with his skill set, yet he gave Belmont credit. "So many great stories—how many strategic missions did you come back from and you were one of the few survivors?" Derby said, alluding to his military career and that as a contractor. Derby picked up his backpack.

Belmont pulled his gun and turned it sideways, pointing it at Derby. The look was one of confusion. Belmont did not even look at him and put his binoculars to his eyes with his other hand. It was his way of telling his friend not to speak and to get down. They both crouched as they watched Charlie and Treble crawl a few feet and station themselves on their elbows within a few yards of the house.

This time, Belmont's and Derby's thoughts were similar. It was unbelievable that they would be thinking about a heist in a neighborhood with this cop in particular. They knew Charlie's band of a few a-holes that everyone had to work around. No real trouble, but not smart enough to realize it and walk away. They smiled to each other. Derby handed Belmont, the better shot, his hunting rifle. They stepped back fifteen feet deeper into the woods. Belmont then took aim with Derby's rifle and fired into the air and above Charlie's head.

The shot was good. It had hit the tree above Charlie. They could run ballistics, but they would not find the hunter or the gun. Belmont thought about shooting again, but saw movement. He watched as Charlie and Treble began to move backwards. He had accomplished what he wanted this time. The two says were retracting.

"Come on Treble. I don't know who it is that fired that shot but I don't think it was random. Someone must have seen us.", said Charlie.

The gunshot was loud. Yet it was nothing for which an officer of the law was not accustomed. Bert opened his door and stepped outside with his coffee in hand. He could see a silhouette of a man or maybe two.

The crack of the rifle was close enough to get everyone's attention, including his neighbors. Charlie hit Treble in the arm, and they backed off Bert's property. When they were far enough to straighten up, they took off through the woods in the other direction. Bert would look at his camera later to see if anyone had been captured by his camera. He stood on his deck confused.

It was the shot of a hunter. He looked to the right and saw shadows running in the distance further into the woods. He looked straight ahead as he knew where the shots must have come from if hunters were on a nearby property or if they were encroaching on his property, his guess. It took a quick second for Bert to figure it out. It had to be a hunter that was aiming for someone who was encroaching on his property, a warning shot against whoever was in the shadows. Bert's hairs on the back of his neck stood up. He walked back into the house as if nothing had happened.

A few minutes passed. Belmont and Derby waited

to make their exit after they felt secure that no one was returning. Bert was down on the first level with his own binoculars to determine if he could see anyone without being seen himself. "There you are, 'shikari,'" said Bert. He saw Belmont and Derby in camouflage. Hunters looking for their prize, but why not just ask, unless they were hunting on private property or on his. He waited long enough to see the men leave.

The mission was in play. There were no more words spoken between them. A mile further back into the woods Belmont and Derby parted their separate ways. Belmont had wished that Bert had investigated. It would have been a clean shot, and he would be that much richer; it would be on to his next play. He would have suffered repercussions for not following the plan, but he would have made a plausible excuse for the both of them.

★★★

The clock showed 5:30 a.m. It was a little earlier than most mornings for Bert. Coffee was on his mind. He had barely slept. It was not due to the hunters in his backyard seeking their prize, his deer. It was the slight pain in his neck which only got worse as he slept. He slept on his back to keep his neck straight. If he turned slightly in either direction, the pain would begin again. It would only get worse from here, he predicted. He would see a doctor after work if he wanted that cortisone shot in the back of his neck. Time would tell how much pain he would be able to endure.

Bert was able to get a better look at his truck in the morning light. He was right; it was not so bad. He could not wait to get to work to see who it was that flicked him off while crashing into him. He was sure that the company for which he drove the truck was insured so his insurance rate would hopefully not go up. As for the driver, he would loose his job and be served a warrant for reckless endangerment and fleeing the scene of an accident.

Sara was the first to greet Bert the next morning. She stood there by the elevator waiting for him to exit. She had seen him on the camera footage entering the building. As he exited, she walked over to him and handed him a coffee. Bert was embarrassed. It was only Jay, his partner, which was laughing. "Are you okay, and how's your truck?" she said as she examined him for scratches.

Not two years old, was his only thought. "I'm okay, it's okay, and thanks for the coffee; I appreciate it," said Bert. "It was a little difficult sleeping last night. I think I pinched a nerve and have a bit of a headache. And before you ask, I will get checked out if I need to at some point. Thanks for your concern." Bert thought he had nipped in the bud whatever concerns Sara might have. *No more conversation* was his only thought, but Sara was still standing in his way. He waited silently, not saying a word, in hopes that there would be no more conversation. She was waiting for him to have a sip of his coffee so he could tell her how he liked it, but he just stood there.

The elevator door opened again and a few people got out and walked around them. "No problem, it's your normal, Verona with honey and cinnamon." Bert was not sure he had a normal, but it was a cup of Joe, and that was a normal for most people.

She wanted to ask him about whether he had thought about her invite, but did not feel like the timing was right. "I am going to take lunch at three today if you would like to join me. We could talk about my invite," she said enthusiastically. They were now attracting more attention. One of his more humorous coworkers raised his eyebrow in a similar fashion to that of the Rock, Dwayne Johnson. He would catch grief later for sure.

The elevator door opened one more time as an officer entered, speaking into his radio. Bert looked down, then back up at Sara and at his watch. Even if he did want to have lunch with Sara, he probably would not be able to last until three. "Well, here's the thing. I am still thinking it over. Email me the information, and I'll let you know tonight or tomorrow."

Detective Captain Murphy, came out of his office and waved Bert to come over. Jay looked over at Murphy, to see if he also would be part of the meeting, but the captain shook his head no. "Just Bert, you and I already talked," said Murphy. Sara assumed that she was being blown off, which was not far from the truth, and began walking back to her unit.

The coffee was no longer hot. "I'll be around if you need anything," she said. Not an unusual statement, as often he needed things to be dispatched, and she was his person, but as for anything personal, he was sure he was not interested. They always had good radio conversation, snarky comments here and there. Then she showed up one night after her shift. It happened that he too was ending his day. They talked for about an hour, and their friendship budded.

The tiresomeness of going to the captain's office to assist in their cases was offset by the results. Bert was both a source for information and deduction as the cop who beat the streets. The streets, his first love, were why he came in early and why he would leave late. He dropped the coffee in a trash can as he headed across the office to the captain's office.

The door was wide open. "Sit down," said Detective Captain Murphy as he walked behind him and shut the door. "I'm not going to offer you any coffee," he said with a wink. "But I'm giving you another shot at detective." He paused. "This case is different." Bert knew that every case according to the captain was different, urgent, and in need of his special care. "This case is vital to a nation's security." Bert looked around as if he was the center of a joke. "Captain Jaks is lending you to us temporarily until this case is closed. We need more than your input, so we've acquired you."

Bert felt like his head was caught in a noose. "So I don't have a choice in the matter, and it really is a matter of national security? You can't figure this out with a whole department of detectives? I am the best?" asked Bert. It just did not make sense. He looked around again as if someone was pulling his leg.

Detective Captain Murphy paced the room for a minute. "Yes, why you are so incredulous I don't understand. You've helped us out on more cases than not, Jay too. I need you, hands-on and present. I would be even more elated if you stayed on as a detective."

The argument was lost. *"Elated"—this is really bad*, thought Bert. Captain Jaks had already said yes, temporarily, so it was not about him saying no but rather about getting it done so he could go back on the streets. "Okay, Detective Captain Murphy, so let me see the case file. I'll give it a few hours and let you know what I think. Who will I be working with, and reporting?" Bert had a no-nonsense manner that came from his strict upbringing.

The captain lifted the blue folder in one hand with his lips pursed and set it down again. The office shades were open. He could see Jay from his desk. He stuck his head out the door and requested Jay's presence. "Jay will be working with you. He is willing to stay at our precinct as a detective. He works for us. I know how you feel about all this, but this is not about feelings as much as facts." He stepped away from his desk.

Jay entered the office, more cavalier than usual. The uniform was still of a police officer, but the attitude of a detective. "What's up, boss?" he said like Bugs Bunny, holding up a pretend cigar. Detective Captain Murphy motioned him to shut the door and sit down. "Did he tell you the news?" he now said addressing Bert. "I'm staying. My family is still moving to a better district with better schools, roads, taxes, and ratings for safety. We are not sure where yet, but I'll commute here."

Bert held the words he knew not to say. He felt like he was being railroaded into something from which he could not turn back.

The room was now quiet. What really made Jay giddy was that he would be working with Bert on this upcoming case. Bert was still looking down, which he did a lot, but managed to give him a nod of approval.

Detective Captain Murphy cleared his throat. "These are the facts. Everything we discuss goes no further than this room. You can be the change." It was the last words that resonated with Bert. The words were a validation that this was where he was supposed to be. *Okay God.*

A change was needed, and a hopelessness had set in for

all. If he was supposed to be here temporarily he would commit a hundred percent. His long-term purpose he still questioned. *Not my will, but Your will be done.*

The red Nespresso machine was behind the captain's desk. Jay pointed to the Nespresso machine. The captain was not sure what he meant. "Coffee, can I get a cup of coffee?" said Jay, which seemed a little bold. The captain said sure and continued speaking. Bert had hoped that Jay would be less distracted, but that was normal.

The once again lifted the blue folder and put it down. "Your clearances are important on this as it goes across the agency. The role as police officer, as you already know, makes you uniquely qualified for this investigation: the working knowledge of the streets, troublemakers, where, when, and how things go down, the court systems, and who the judges and prosecutors are is essential." He paused and smiled. He waited for Jay to finish with his coffee. Detective Captain Murphy had wanted to have Bert become part of his team for almost as long as he was captain.

Two cups of coffee were in Jay's hands as he walked back to the chairs in front of Detective Captain Murphy's desk. He handed one to Bert. "Thank you, you too Sara." said Bert and stopped himself. He appreciated the straight cup of coffee hot, much more than the other.

It would take some time before the detective captain

would be completely comfortable with Bert and Jay. "Especially and specifically," Murphy said, "your credibility in court and on the street has made the biggest difference locally. The clearances I had Jaks, Captain Jaks, put in for the both of you last month came at the request of the FBI. Jay, you already had your clearances in order, so we don't have to wait on yours to be expedited. This is an outside movement, not sure of the funding. It targets certain high-level personnel within organizations." He paused for a moment. He wanted to say 'Who abide in darker realms.' but opted for something more palatable. "Their movement that is highly funded is assassinating police officers and other officials. It's an attempt to have certain areas cave to their local militias, my own term."

Bert and Jay looked at each other and laughed. It was a joke, and they both got it. Bert looked around for cameras. They were the police officers that only belonged on the street, and detectives matter most. "Okay, we get it," Jay said and pushed back his chair to stand.

The door was a few feet away, but the captain sprang for it. He stood in front of the door, not letting either Bert or Jay leave. "Not a joke; it is as real as can be. Don't you watch the news? None of this is over. You both have had at least top secret clearances, so you are aware of how clearances work. This is unclassified information that you can look over, but it still remains in this room," said Detective Captain Murphy.

Bewildered, Jay froze. He did not agree to give out any information with full clearances. The captain once again motioned for him to sit down as he went back to his desk.

The folder sat on Bert's lap. "Is this the only version we are going to get?" he asked. He really wanted to say that this was over his pay grade. His life had just been made even more complicated. He wanted the right thing to happen but still for things to stay simple, *but maybe the two don't go together*, he thought sadly.

Jay opened his folder and started to notice a certain pattern. "No, we're waiting for your clearance to come through today; then there will be more intel after that," said Detective Captain Murphy. "You will be meeting with two agents who are already working on this. Different states and cities have different problems. Certain states and cities which have already withdrawn large amounts of funding for law enforcement have certain institutions up for grabs and more criminal activities. The more lucrative the economy, the more coveted and susceptible to infiltration. We also are investigating criminal activity that has been incited by this organization against local authorities. According to the paper trail, everyone wants a piece of the action." The captain had their full attention. They were captivated.

★★★

The coffee was brewed. Pauline was ready to finish up her first chapter. Still in her pj's, her demeanor had changed. She was no longer excited about what she was writing. It was going too slowly. She reverted back to an outline and no longer romanticized about her typewriter.

The typewriter had been pushed aside for her computer. She really wanted it to work but realized that for her to have the perfect writing environment, she needed not only the retro-looking typewriter but also a room with a view: a room in a Victorian bungalow that overlooked the ocean from not only her balcony but also the kitchen. While she had her house up on that cliff, there might as well be one of those white fluffy cats that she could hold while it purred after she finished one of her novels. So the typewriter would not do without the view.

Praise and worship … where did she leave off? Kara, her sweet-hearted character, was finding her own answers to the dark day and age in which they now lived. She read the ancient stories of the Old Testament in the Bible. She found that it was similar to what she had gone through in her city. Her city and country had been uprooted so quickly and without mercy.

It seemed to have been almost overnight as she thought through the events. The understanding she had was simple. There was always something that they were doing against God, whether it was worshipping idols, killing their children, letting a woman be raped, or some other form of evil. They had to repent, turn back, and once again trust in Him. Trust in His words and promises and be sorry. They always had to repent because God always accounted for everything.

The pages seemed too daunting. She began to click again.

> Kara started to understand. It was never creation, but rather God. The ruin that was around her was not what God wanted her to see. "Thank You, God. I'm sorry for not paying attention. I'll worship only You," she whispered.

The first chapter ended. Pauline thought it was a good place to end as Kara, her tender-hearted woman, was not sure that she understood but was willing to step out in faith and pray. She reflected on what she typed and liked "Thank You, God." She lifted up her own thanks with a very grateful heart.

Pauline wondered if she should include the verse about the Samaritan where Jesus describes worship of the Jewish people versus the Samaritans and then that of the Christian.

> Jesus said to her, "Woman, believe Me, the hour is coming when you will neither on this mountain, nor in Jerusalem,

worship the Father. You worship what
you do not know; we know what we
worship, for salvation is of the Jews. But
the hour is coming, and now is, when the
true worshipers will worship the Father in
spirit and truth; for the Father is seeking
such to worship Him. God is Spirit, and
those who worship Him must worship in
spirit and truth." (John 4:21–24)

The book was coming together. She thought about it
and would put it in at a later time in the story. The story
was starting to evolve, *Worship and praise*, she thought.
She included characters that had appeared in some of her
previous stories. She started to reread some of her novel
and realized it was missing something. She was not sure
what it was yet, but it would come to her after she prayed
a little more about it.

Her life also was coming into shape. She reflected on
praise and worship and how that was key not in a self-help
way but as an ultimate truth, an absolute. We are created
as human beings to worship; what we choose to worship
is what defines us. Pauline had not thought about it that
way until she read the verse. Jesus came to heal us of our
transgressions, restore us, build us up, and give us life
abundantly. We can worship nothing but Jesus if He is the
ultimate truth and our own internal spirit testifies to it.

> Jesus answered, "I am the way and the
> truth and the life. No one comes to the
> Father except through Me. If you had
> known Me, you would know My Father
> as well. From now on you do know Him
> and have seen Him." (John 14:6–7)

Jesus is the reason. Pauline's life was centered. How great is it to be able to worship something that is not going to falter and is not imperfect? Anything less than holy is not going to cut it. It is good to worship a holy God and just let go.

The next few hours were eventful. The text read, *I am still buried in things that I need to get done. I have a new job, but within the same spectrum. Thank you for the thank-you card. I was hoping to stop by tonight if you are not too busy.*

The next text was different. It was *I am right outside.* Pauline grabbed her robe and went to the dining room window to see, but was surprised to see another man standing on her front step. She opened the door and welcomed Seth. "Oh, sorry if I seemed surprised, but I thought that you were my neighbor. I am not sure how I could have gotten your texts confused," she said, looking at her phone and then looking around the corner.

It was too early for visitors. "It's not too early, is it?" asked Seth. "You're still in your PJs. It must be nice to have a day off.", said Seth. "It's also my day off, so I thought I would go for a run and then stop by on my way back. In a way we both are a little undone, since I am little sweaty." She did not notice when she had first invited him in, but now she realized he was dripping with sweat.

The water bottle was half-full. "Thanks for stopping by. It's great seeing you again," she said awkwardly. "Can I fill your water bottle?" She realized at once how dumb the question was. It was almost as dumb as telling someone new to church that they can stop by any time since they live nearby.

Seth looked at his bottle and shook his head no. He had never shied away from anything in his life and was not about be deterred by awkward conversation. "Hey, Pauline, I really appreciate you introducing yourself at church. I think I could go there again. I thought maybe I could pick you up a little later on this afternoon and take you out for lunch and we could talk about it."

She looked at her phone and thought about Bert's text. *It's all about timing*, she thought, *but then again I could be a little more careful when reading my texts.* He wiped his forehead with a towel. "It's Seth, right?" she asked. He nodded. "Sure, but I have to run some errands so I'll meet you somewhere. Is that okay?"

The towel went back into his side pocket. "Sure, that's fine. It'll be some place around here. I was thinking of that pizza place over by the hardware shop. I'll text you the address and time." She agreed. As he left, she began to reread her texts. His had come in right after Bert's? It was embarrassing; she could not wait to tell Bert.

The rest of the morning was uneventful. She ate, showered and dressed. She was hoping to start back in on her new chapter but decided to leave it until after lunch. Seth seemed like a nice guy. It would be a good idea to introduce Bert to Seth; maybe they would hit it off.

Chapter Four

· ·

Whatever This Is

*L*ater that afternoon, Seth met Pauline at the pizza place. She ordered a salad; Seth laughed. She just did not look like the type to eat only a salad. "What's so funny?" she asked. "I'll also have a slice of cheese pizza." She pulled out her wallet and waited.

The receipt was left on the counter. Any other time he would have waited for the other person to pick it up unless, it was someone he was trying to impress. She was someone with whom he would make a good impression. He would have to intentionally be lame before he could disappoint Pauline. Part of his profession was sizing up people up quickly. She was uptight, probably lonely, no standards as far dating and zero personality. He had this date in the bag.

Pauline opened her wallet and pulled out a few dollars. "No," he said. "I really appreciate you meeting with me. I don't know anyone here. It seems like a very welcoming area, so I am sure in time I'll meet the right person or people." He gently pushed her hand back with the money. "I am a little concerned about the crime rate, but other than that, the property values are rising, schools are good, and developers are building. Where we live in our zip code and surrounding zip codes it seems to be safe, but outside of this area crimes are hitting new heights."

There was an isolated table near the front of the pizzeria. They took a seat. It was later in the afternoon when fewer people were in the restaurant, so they almost had the place to themselves. Seth was more comfortable around fewer people. He watched Pauline fish through her purse. He figured she was looking for her phone or her wallet.

The phone was on top of her car keys and wallet. "Ah," she said and retrieved a business card in the front of her wallet. "Here, it's a business card for my cousin, Sam, but it's not really for Sam. She is engaged and quite busy these days." said Pauline. "It's for my friend, Bert. You must have thought I had only one friend, but I have two, if you can count my cousin as my friend." She nearly blushed at her own attempt at humor. "I'm crossing out her information and writing Bert's on the back of this card. He knows this town better than most. He is always looking to welcome people into our neighborhood."

The card showed Sam's information with a line through but still legible. He flipped it over and put it in his plaid shirt pocket. Pauline was not used to guys dressing so preppy. "Thanks, I'll call Sam tonight," he said. She rolled her eyes. "For a second, I thought you were trying to set me up with someone," he said, waiting for her reaction. She showed none. "See, it's like this. I just came off a serious relationship, and I am not interested in just anyone." He reached for the pen next to her hand. She thought he was reaching for her hand and slightly brushed up against it. The thought crossed her mind that it might have been intentional. He tore off a part of the card and wrote his number on it.

The pizza came and was set on a stand between them. The salad and a piece of cheese pizza was placed in front of Pauline. Seth handed her back the torn card with his number. "Give this to your cousin. Oops, I mean Bert, so he can call me, just in case he misses my call." She put it in her purse to give to Bert later.

The pizza smelled like New York pizza should. She took another two slices together and laid them on the paper plate. *That's more like it*, Seth thought. He was a good judge of character; nothing surprised him about Pauline. She definitely was not the dainty or down-home type, but a cross of the two. She was more precisely plain Jane.

She was taking a bite when he asked about Bert. "He lives nearby and mostly keeps to himself. So if you hang out with him, it would be as good for him as you," she said with her mouth still a little full but hiding it behind her hand as she spoke. She made him sound like he was in need of guy friends, which was not true, but she left it at that. "Do you want some salad?" she asked.

71

The salad was slid into the middle of the table like the pizza. In truth that was all he wanted, but he shook his head no and took another bite of his pizza. "So what does Bert do for a living, or is he retired?" Despite shaking his head no at first, Seth helped himself to a full plate of salad. "Sure you don't mind?" was his rhetorical question. He took one of the vinaigrette packets and poured it on his salad. *Health nut*, she figured; *right*. But she did not care and just enjoyed her third piece of pizza.

The pizza place was getting more crowded. She looked at her watch and then answered, "He's kind of in between jobs right now." She had forgotten to text him back after his earlier text, but had a feeling that his job needed to be anonymous.

Seth was a little annoyed at this non-answer. "Well, what kind of field is he in, unless you would rather not say? We all have our secrets."

The table next to them had four children who were well behaved and very talkative. They talked about what "dodging the point" meant with their parents. She eavesdropped on their conversation, amused. She looked around to see if she recognized anyone, which she did not. Her dentist was right next door and normally would stop in to say hi, but she needed to get back. "It's more that I would rather you have something to talk about with him," she said. She looked at her watch again. "I've got to be going, but thank you. This has been a real treat." She stood up.

He was uncomfortable with her leaving before him. He used a diversion tactic to get her to stay. He chose to take advantage of the same nearby kids. They were annoying but tolerable. Seth made a funny face at the littlest one in the highchair. She made a face back. "Cute, how old?" he asked the mother.

"She is only two and a half.", replied the mother. Pauline was standing up with both hands on her purse in front of her. She could see Seth had a personable side. She smiled at the mother. She was handed a box by the owner of the restaurant which she placed on the table.

The owner of the pizzeria asked Pauline if everything was all right. "Yes, it is always great. You know this is my favorite place for pizza, bar none," she said. He had his hands folded across his apron and nodded for an introduction. She was obliged to do so. She introduced the owner to Seth.

The chair slid backward and he stood up. "Blessed to meet you. This is a wonderful establishment. You not only serve great pizza, but your salad is really tasty. Not sure how you get iceberg lettuce to taste like that.", said Seth shaking his hand.

He usually fixed his meals at home and was always learning new ways to cook or preserve things. The owner laughed until he realized he was serious and remarked it was locally grown. He then walked over to the next table.

Pauline still stood there in front of him with her purse in front of her. She lifted her right hand and waved, which was ungainly, as she had become self-conscious. "Thank you again for this. It was wonderful to get out of the house. I'm still thinking virus and stay home more than I go out.", she said. "I'm glad everyone is still distancing themselves from others by a few feet and tables being spread apart. It may give us hope for whatever is lurking around the corner." It was a sad thought, as most people no longer talked about it. It was a sullen moment.

The unhappiness of the virus did not strike Seth as it did others. Nevertheless a wave of sympathy for her swept over him. "I enjoyed our date, even if you have to leave." he said. She felt it too and was taken aback at the sudden connection. The awkwardness of the moment was lingered. *Date*, what was she to do with that? She had not thought about a date but knew it was not. If it was a date, she would have remained at the table for a little longer.

The box on the table was no longer empty as she started to fill it with pizza and then salad. She was bright crimson. The thought of sitting back down crossed her mind. She looked at the chair but did not unclasp the box. Another time, she thought.

The words came quick. "It's just we were both done eating at the time," she said. "Thank you for whatever this is, sincerely. I'm sorry for leaving so abruptly. I need to get home, but thank you." She was not sure what to make of what had just happened, but she did not want to overthink it, but *plus-one* came to her mind.

★★★

That night there was an orange moon. She half-teased Bert, pointing out that the moon was foreboding and that they should put off getting together for another night. Bert pointed out that his day could not get any worse; he was still reeling from his accident, and everything was being shaken. Tonight he needed solace and a friend. On a lighter note, she said that as Christians, they were not affected by omens anyway.

Bert arrived with a bottle of merlot from a local winery and gave Pauline a kiss on her cheek. A kiss from a friend, she qualified, as she had other thoughts since lunch that made her question any of her other emotions. She took the bottle of wine and thanked him for that and the kiss.

The savor of dinner filled his senses as soon as the door was opened. It was chicken and mushrooms in a white wine sauce, herbed roasted potatoes, fresh buns, and asparagus or a salad, if he were to bet. "Our favorite," he said without hesitating. "What is it, chicken and potatoes?" His day had been grueling; she had no idea how hard it was to be jovial. However, a good dinner and a great companion would put him on a path of healing.

Life was depressing right now. The only thing this week he was looking forward to was prepping his deer, cutting it up, storing it, and eating it. One breath at a time, he reminded himself. He did not expect anyone to understand. Pauline was the exception; she could make sense of what he was thinking and feeling. Except when he was beside her, he stood alone.

The house was toasty, especially as they walked toward the kitchen. She opened the oven to show him. "Lucky guess," she said. He was right. There was the chicken with mushrooms, herbed potatoes, and asparagus. The buns were on the oven but had not gone in yet. She slid the roll of buns onto the lower rack and turned the temperature down before closing the oven. She was always glad to have company for dinner. She gave him a side hug. "It's good to see you again," she said in a friendly tone. He grunted as she hugged him and put her head against his shoulder.

They ate slowly and discussed much. "I am not sure about this promotion to detective. The pro is that I get to work with Jay. He has already accepted the promotion. It's not what I want, but I don't have a choice for the short term. I was not really even asked," he said; "I was acquired."

She rose to get the bottle of wine. Had she known it was going to be one of these nights she would have prepared herself a little better and not have scheduled any phone calls for later. She wrote texts to her editor and publisher the she would have to push back their meetings until next week. They would not be happy, but when were they ever happy?

The bottle was a cabernet. The year was 2022. "This is okay?", asked Pauline and showed Bert the bottle.

The year was not a good for a Napa wine. The preference was for an aged wine, but Pauline never knew. Bert nodded. "Fine,", he said and continued to talk about his new position. Their wine selection was never aged or collected. The goal was to have a bottle or two on reserve if there was a reason or a special occasion.

The bottle was opened and the glasses were poured. "It sounds a bit complicated. They need you for an interdepartmental case that is classified. The case is important?" said Pauline. Her mind was going a hundred miles a minute. It would be great story material. She wondered why it was that they had to go to such a level as to acquire Bert and Jay.

The wine swished, it was smelt and then tasted. "I am sure short-term this is where I am suppose to be, this case. Longterm, no one even knows what this job or department is going to look like. It's a new organization with no proven results. Meanwhile, I do a good job as a cop and with results."

Bert acquiesced because he was needed. His duty and loyalty resided in something bigger than his own preference. Pauline wanted to ask several more questions.

She thought about how classified the case might be. "Are you sure you are supposed to be telling me any of this?" she asked. She worried for him and his naiveté.

The wine was smooth. "This is pretty good for a California wine. You can taste the black cherry, without it being too fruity.", he said. "I wondered about the year.", he said. Wine usually put him to sleep if he shared more than one bottle.

The glasses were lifted. There was a silent toast. "It's good.", she said and took another gulp. Pauline did not drink except for special occasions, but this was the exception. Although it was not a celebration, she thought it would be appropriate since he was being promoted.

The thought about propriety crossed his mind. "For a starter, don't give out my information to anyone and everything I just said is to be kept quiet, only the two of us, right?" said Bert. "Things are different now, but not between us." He was not sure why he added "not between us."

Pauline was caught off guard. "I gave your number out today to Seth, a newcomer to our church. He recently moved into a nearby neighborhood and is in need of fellowship. I did not tell him what you did for a living, but he asked. I only told him that you were in between jobs," said Pauline. "That's okay, isn't it? Oh, wait here for a second." She quickly left the table and retrieved the number that he had given her. She handed it to Bert.

The number was on the small torn piece of Sam's business card. "This is hard on the eyes. It looks like it was written in gibberish. Can you make it out?" asked Bert.

No was the answer. Pauline shook her head and left the table once more. She returned with her smart-phone. The phone had to be adjusted so it focused on the right part of the paper. She laughed as it took a little while to do what should have been a simple task.

Their heads were touching. The magnifier attribute of her phone clearly showed the number and name. "Seth Cooper, 408-772-4230, so it seems. He is a nice guy. At first I thought he was a little off, insecure. He actually was more confident than I thought." Bert held the card and gave her a sidelong glance. Pauline could tell she had made a mistake.

He handed the card back to her. "If he is going to call me, I'll wait," he said. He was not sure how to work the next question so he decided to be bold. "Were you on a date?" The pain in his neck shot down as he tried to turn his head to look at her directly. "Do you have any Advil?" He asked and rubbed his neck.

The medicine cabinet was upstairs. She did not want to leave the table without an explanation. It had to be casual. She remembered that she had a packet of Advil that she kept in her purse. "Of course, give me a second." She picked her purse off of the cabinet and searched through it for her Advil. "I'm not sure," she said, thinking about whether she wanted it to be a date. "He said it was, but I had no idea what it was. I went to leave, and then he said, 'Thank you for the date.' It was unexpected." She handed the Advil to Bert.

He took the packet and looked up at her. "You were leaving? Okay, the meeting was intentional. So you thought you were just going to tell him about church, so what did you tell him? Can I get some water? Never mind, sorry, I can get it myself." She made a face.

She had handed him her water she had with dinner but had not finished. "No, I can see you're hurt, you should let me do things for you." She paused. "I know, I can do your trash for you tonight," she said enthusiastically. He shook his head. She realized that she avoided his original question. "We never talked about church other than he was glad that I had introduced myself to him. We talked about other things. He really needs a friend, and so do you. I am not sure if he's going to keep coming to church or not, but that can't be helped."

The friend that he needed was now sitting opposite him. She sat down across from Bert so he would not have to turn his head. "Not your worry," said Bert. "Keep me informed, and I'll keep his number and call him later this week. Thank you." He had the small piece of the business card in his hand. If he put it in his pocket he most likely would find it in the wash at a later time, so he put it in his wallet instead.

They continued to talk for the rest of the evening. The moon was mesmerizing. They talked in the sunroom while they played cards, discussing everything from politics to her new book. They looked up at the orange moon and wondered if it would always remain so beautiful.

★★★

The night was still young. Belmont lay back in his chair and rotated his monitor with his foot. He had been working two jobs. In one he had more autonomy. The other was for the officer who'd strung up a deer in his backyard. One took duplicity and skill, while the other paid less and was easier.

It figured for an old-time sheriff who lived out in the country, but that was not Bert. He was a straight-laced police officer who got more satisfaction out of just being there for the people he served than any police officer he'd ever met, including those on film. He did not feel bad about killing him; he just found him to be fashioned out of a different mold than most people. He make a gun with his fingers and pulled the trigger at the monitor.

The tropical island background portrayed on the monitor—with families eating, people walking, and a certain man reading a newspaper watching people coming and going—could have been in a painting or at least a postcard. No orange moon, Belmont contended in his

81

mind. The tropical islands have nothing on this place, he said satirically.

That imaginary gun was pointed at the man who read his newspaper. He lowered his newspaper as if he knew he was being watched and surveyed his surroundings. If someone located his whereabouts, there would be no escaping either the satellite imagery or whatever other means by which they found him. He had been on the run too long with no places left to hide. There would be no other identities to take and no other disguises that he would be able to muster. It would take a small miracle to help him escape this time. His own genius had quit. He lifted up his finger at the invisible man and went back to reading his newspaper.

Belmont shrugged. He retrieved a picture from his printer. It was Pauline. Most people might find her attractive, but he was not sure yet. There was something simplistic in her mannerisms that were more matronly than most women. She dressed and looked as if she had stepped out of a fifties magazine. It was the mod appearance of unique clothing and hairstyle. An odd duck for sure, he thought, plain Jane, semi-attractive, not his type.

The computer showed a caller, Chas Ward. Belmont picked up. "Charlie, you got my message. Hey, was that you and a friend outside of Officer Channing's house, last night?" he asked. There was silence. "Don't hang up. I am as guilty as you are. Can we meet? Okay, texting you information, and I'll meet you."

Charlie was shaking. He would go alone. Somehow trouble had a way of finding him, or he had a way of finding it. Either way he was having second thoughts. It was Grandma. She kept coming back to him in memories but mostly in love, in an unconditional way. She was not disappointed in him; it was something else. His grandparents were a sacred memory.

A good choice is a stepping stone and a bad choice can be like quick-sand. It was a choice at a time that eventually led him to forget the precious memories that he had held on to so tightly growing up. The hope that there would be something better for him someday, something reminiscent of their house and home. The presence he had felt growing up comprised feelings of security, holiness, and love.

It was the very thing he found at Pauline's home. It did not smell of pies, bread, or cinnamon and apples or cedar the way it did as you climbed the stairs at Grandma's, but it was the same. He thought hard about what it could be that would have brought him back to his younger years. Grandma always talked about angels. Maybe her house was filled with …. He stopped himself and put his head in his hands. How far he had fallen to be talking about angels and Grandma? He stood up to go, putting on his jacket.

The Sonic was well lit up when he arrived. Anywhere else Belmont would have preferred, but assumed Charlie was a fan, as his informant put him here with Lucy more times than not. He hoped this would go smoothly but was not betting on it. Belmont watched him walk onto the property. "Charlie, I'm Belmont. It's good to meet you." He walked him over to a place where they could not be heard. "Want you to know I'm a fan. You showing up there at night to scout out the place was top-notch, but I am not sure he has anything worth stealing." He continued. "I heard you are looking for work. I'm not sure what you are thinking, but I may have something for you."

The feeling that Charlie received while hanging out with Belmont was close to the feeling he got when he was hanging out with Stern, but Belmont looked a lot smarter and was a hell of lot older. He was more fit as well. In short sleeves you could see he was very muscular, probably a health fanatic. He probably had it together, whatever he was managing. "Thanks, I think," said Charlie. "You're not a cop?"

Belmont wanted to tell him what he was doing was not the caliber that would put him on anybody's radar, but he just said no. The gun behind Charlie's back could get him in trouble if he did not have a carry permit, but Belmont didn't say anything. Poor urchin, must be a little scared. "Hey, I don't want you to do anything that would make you feel uncomfortable," said Belmont. Charlie felt like he might have said that a little too often and hoped no one fell for it. It gave him the heebie-jeebies.

The waitress who came to the car in front of them gave them a dirty look until she recognized Charlie. She immediately smiled and waved. "Hey, did you need anything?" she yelled. *Yep, he is a regular*, Belmont thought. Charlie waved her on to go. "All right, but you let me know."

The attention was not what Charlie wanted, and he was starting to get agitated. "Not to cut you short, but you said we were the same. What did you mean? We were just following the deer. That was the same as you?" asked Charlie. "Your voicemail sounded like you had something on me. That's why I called you back."

The waitresses coming and going out of Sonic all seemed to be about the same age. A couple decades younger than him but only about five years younger than Charlie. They all seemed to notice him. "Well, I was hoping you would not mind keeping tabs on somebody—or two somebodies." He pulled out a picture of Pauline. "It would be five grand to start and five grand at the end."

The picture was current. Charlie was angry, but he could not understand why. "Yeah, what do you want me to do? I barely know her." He regretted having said that. He knew he would be asked too many questions.

Belmont picked up the picture and studied it. "You know her, how?" he asked. It was finally getting interesting.

Charlie wanted to grab the picture back but let him hold on to it for now. "I was there at her house. I was casing it and realized like you said there was nothing there," said Charlie. "I went on to the next house and that's when you saw me. You shot that bullet over my head." Although that was not true, it was good enough for Belmont to believe. They were there to see what he could find out about the officer who he met at Pauline's house. He and Treble almost took a tour of the house since he left only the screen door locked, but they noticed the backyard camera.

The picture of Pauline was placed directly in front of Charlie. "You're a bright, like a star.", said Belmont dotingly. Charlie could only think of Belmont as haughty. A word his grandma used to describe something that love was not, that and prideful. *Love is never haughty or selfish or rude. It does not hold grudges and will hardly even notice when others do it wrong.* If he was right, it was somewhere in First Corinthians 13. He may have left out parts, but he remembered it!

Bible verses—they were coming to his mind. It wasn't the first since his encounter with Pauline. At first he could not believe it came back to him after all this time. Then he realized his mind was filling up with Bible verses.

He had to get Grandma out of his head, or his head would be toast, and yet here he is being asked to spy on someone who speaks grandma in an uncanny way. He felt as though he was being choked.

Once again he studied Pauline's picture. "You know not to act like you know me if we run into each other.", said Belmont. Charlie agreed. "What I need you to do, as long as you left it on good terms, is to be someone who needs work. Offer to work only on the outside of the house if need be so as not to scare her. Tell her how desperately you need the work. She should eventually agree to something.", Belmont looked at his phone. Mr. Newspaper man was on the move, probably going back to his hotel.

Charlie shook his head yes, ten grand for betraying someone more dubious than himself, this guy. "Sounds good, everything is doable from my end.", said Charlie. Somehow he would warn Pauline of whatever Belmont's true intentions were. "I think she likes me."

The phone was still Belmont's focus. "You have a puppy dog mentality to you," Belmont said now, looking up. "I just want to pet you and look I am throwing you a bone. It's a ten-K bone! You should first ask Bert if you can do something for him, just to grease the wheels."

That was a good idea, but Charlie hated that it was coming from this guy. He was creepy, and he rarely thought that about anyone. "When do I get my—" Charlie started to ask, but the envelope was slid before him. Belmont placed the picture of Pauline on top.

The envelope was not thick. He did not count it but put it in his jacket pocket. "If you are missing any of it, just let me know. I usually know how to count.", said Belmont. Charlie took it back out and checked that it was all there. He did not want to be in bad form. Charlie did not have to ask when the final payment would be.

The newspaper man had vanished completely. "What if something doesn't go as planned?", asked Charlie. He figured Belmont was only accessible when he wanted to be which could be tricky.

A phone was slid across the table. "It's untraceable. I'll be the one to be in touch with you but if you have to call me get rid of the phone afterwards.", said Belmont. "No other calls please, Chas Ward and me. You to me and me to you, is the function of this phone. This only involves you, not Lucy or Treble. Also I think Stern isn't a team player. Think about that."

The orange moon was brilliant. Five grand in his pocket, just like that. It was too easy, but he would not complain. He told Belmont so long and held up his new phone, saying, "We'll be in touch." He texted Lucy that he would be over in the morning and would not be checking in tonight, adding emojis for a sleepyhead and prayer hands. Then it occurred to him that she would be up all night trying to figure out what it meant, so he typed it out: *Sleep well and say your prayers.*

His phone vibrated as he got to his car. He pulled out his car keys. It was Lucy. He turned around to see where Belmont was, but he was nowhere to be seen. "Hey, Lucy. Sorry, just wanted to let you know I was okay, but am going to bed," said Charlie. "I thought you might not get the emojis that I had sent, so I wrote it out for you so you were not up all night trying to figure out what I meant by it."

The car started, but as he went to close the door, Belmont was standing between him and the door. "One last thing. Before I say anything, is that Lucy?" Belmont asked. Charlie nodded.

Lucy was panicked. "Who's there?" she asked. "Are you at that meeting?" She looked again at her message and was sure Charlie was in trouble. "Charlie, can you stop by here on your way home?" Charlie said he would and he would call her back on his way.

It was the way he said *one last thing* that was not okay. Charlie was scared; he peed himself a trickle. He had already put his gun beside him in the console when he took a seat. He was glad he had Lucy on the phone. She was probably tracing his last Google location.

Belmont said, "Just wanted to let you know not to pursue Bert or Pauline on your own for any reason. So the ten grand in essence is to stop anything you and your crew were planning. Got it?"

For once Charlie thought Belmont sounded normal instead of something out of a horror film. Charlie nodded again and waited for him to walk away from the car before pulling out. He did not want to have Belmont magically appear in his backseat with "One last thing." He had the chills driving away from the Sonic.

Sonic and the big orange moon were in the background. Strange night indeed. "Hey, Lucy, are you okay?" he asked. He looked down at his jeans for his pee spot but did not see anything. "I'll be there in a few, but I can't stay long."

The timing was good. Charlie arrived at Lucy's house within twenty minutes. He parked on the street. The house was small and the floor plan simple, but it suited Lucy. It was only eleven hundred square feet, the size of a large apartment, but it was on Main Street. There was a college nearby. The restaurants and shops were inundated with business from the foot traffic. It was a fun place to live, with a large lake, hiking trails, and bike paths nearby. Charlie did not particularly like the place, especially compared to his house, which was deep in the woods and surrounded by trees and a river.

The walkway to her home was old cobblestone and well kept. Her father wanted to make sure that no one would trip and injure themselves on the walkway or the steps, so he had it maintained monthly by a landscaping company, which also took care of the front and back yards of the property. Lucy told her father she had insurance for those type of incidents, but he was a cop who was used to taking precautions. Lucy said it was just another excuse for him to be in her life.

Lucy's dad had worked in the same precinct as Bert before he divorced and moved away. She made little reference to their family, but Charlie was sure that they helped finance the old brick slab house, probably out of guilt. Their divorce was hard on Lucy, like Charlie's mom's lifestyle. Charlie's mom never needed an excuse to drop him off somewhere, the mall or a friend's house since she had something to do most of the time. As soon as he was ten she stopped leaving him with people.

It was what they bonded over as children. They would go down by the water and skip stones and talk about their families. They were closer when they were younger. Charlie had been to her house on several occasions before her parents split and her dad moved to Texas. It was his mom's favorite place to drop him off. Although Charlie would tell her he was too old to be dropped off at a friend's house, his mom would still drop him whether he was friends with them or not. She would also pick him up late, especially if she was on a date. It was embarrassing. Lucy's was a happy home, or so he thought; at least he liked it better than his own.

Lucy's mom and Charlie's mom had become fast friends, the only one of Charlie's mom's friends who was female. Charlie always warned Lucy that she would be a bad influence on her mother. Lucy said her mom had her own ways and would not let anyone influence her. It was hard to say what exactly happened to make her mom and dad separate, but Charlie always thought that his mom had something to do with it. They went out together on occasion, so Lucy's dad would watch the both of them. They explained to Lucy that sometimes people just don't get along, and it's nobody's fault. He remembered Lucy told him it was a lie, but Charlie just shrugged it off. He was sad and maybe disillusioned when they divorced and her dad moved away.

Charlie approached the steps and saw Lucy through the screen door. The door creaked as it opened, and Lucy rushed out and hugged him. He could not remember the last time she had hugged him. It had to be when they were kids. "Are you okay?" asked Charlie.

"I could not make sense of your text," Lucy said. "I was worried. I googled your whereabouts."

The hug lasted forever. She talked as she lay on his shoulder. He kissed the side of her hair. "You did good. I knew you would," said Charlie.

Lucy pushed him back, mad. Charlie was confused. "Why did you do that thing?" she asked. "What is wrong with you? You aren't acting like yourself at all. You've gone all, I don't know what. It's something, something soft, something mushy."

Charlie turned around, walked back to his car, and took off. He would have given her the finger but he did not feel like making up. That would have set everything in Lucille's universe back in order, but he refused. Man, he hated women, sometimes. *Why did she'd have make things weird?*

It wasn't complicated. He did not mean anything by it. It was natural, she was there for him. He could always count on Lucy. He'd known it since they were kids, so why was that so strange? He realized that a month ago he would not have done something like that, so maybe it was that he was maturing or it could be something else. She did say he was getting soft. That must have been it, but it was hard to tell. It would take at least a night before she would be willing to talk to him again.

Lucy stood on her front porch and watched him drive away. That was more than fine. She had only invited him over so she would know for sure that he was okay. Now she wished she hadn't; she was infuriated. He ruined everything.

The phone was now the enemy. She had the incriminating evidence on her phone. It was not just the text but also the compliment: "You did good." People are good or rotten, but they do well or poorly. It was all wrong, whether it came down to an adverb or an adjective. She did not need him telling her that she did well. She knew she did well; everyone does well mostly. She pined for those words usually, like the praise of a father, but when she actually did something, not because she cared. Charlie was like a brother, and of course she cared; she could not help thinking of what her life would have been like had she moved to Texas with her father instead of staying with her mother.

It had been a hard decision, since she was a daddy's girl, but she would have had to leave behind all of her friends and good schools. There was also the fact that her mom needed her the most. She was a mess without her, with no one to manage her money. She started spending money like it was going out of style. From the first time Lucy saw a bill that sat unattended on the counter, she knew her mother was in trouble, so she took over her mother's finances. She warned her that even with the alimony payment and a part-time job, she'd go broke.

That was not the only problem. It was as if her mother had become the teenager, and she was the adult. Her mother lost a ton of weight and went down to a size six, the same size Lucy wore.

It was fun at first before crazy set in. It was the outfits. She had new outfits with new matching boots that Lucy would on occasion be allowed to borrow, but her mother wore her clothes on a regular basis. It was like they were friends and no longer mother and daughter. She talked about her boyfriends and misgivings. Lucy was a good listener.

The counseling part was hard. Her mother now confided in her about everything, including her marriage to her father. Lucy was not sure which parent had the first affair, but clearly they both had been at fault. Her mother had lost it, mentally. She was a different person now.

Charlie had been right. His mother was a bad influence. They would go to bars at night and talk to different strangers. She even started to do drugs, something both she and Charlie swore was something from which they would eternally stay away. They tried weed later in life when it was legalized, but it still was something they did not want in their bodies.

Memories, it was a cold October night, near the end of their marriage, when Lucy realized their family had fallen apart and was beyond repair. Her father had her go into the bar while he waited outside, to spy on her mom and tell her to come home. Her mother shoed her away. Her and Charlie's mom agreed she would be home when she came home. None of it, though, was Charlie's fault.

People are responsible for their own sins. Both moms were in the wrong. Eventually, Lucy's mother got wise and changed her tune. She started to go to church and was a lot less fun. She started to put down strict rules and guidelines by which she had already been abiding.

A new way of life was a push in a new direction. Lucy started to dislike her mother and could not wait to move out. She too took on a new persona of her own. Her grades dropped. She started to steal from small stores that did not have a lot of cameras. She was very good at it. She would lift something right in front of the manager's face while she smiled and talked with him.

Later in life, it became less of a challenge and more of a game in which she had the advantage. Never forgetting she could get caught, she weighed her choice of what she was taking versus what would be the penalty if she could not talk her way out of pressing charges. The bigger the item, the cleverer she got.

There was a time she took pieces of furniture at an estate home sale. She drove a truck into the driveway and loaded priceless furniture. She even had some individuals help load her new pieces of furniture into the truck. The owners of the furniture were coming back to get their furniture at a later time, but she was quicker. She pretended to be their daughter. How did these people know whether the owners had a daughter who would come earlier than expected? She started to feel guilty, but why now? she wondered. That was a job of which she was most proud.

The truck was not hers either, since she was good at spotting an old stray she could hot-wire or a truck with the keys left in the ignition. It was more common with trucks than with passenger vehicles. The truck would be ditched later, and since her fingerprints were not on file, she never worried about getting caught. Although Charlie's mother might have been a bad apple, Lucy could hardly hold his mother's influence against Charlie. After all, it was after her mom turned "good" that Lucy started her life of crime, and she was the one who was responsible for dragging Charlie into a life of thievery, but that was later in life.

The best scores were always around the holidays when no one was paying attention. These thefts were one-stop shops. She and Charlie would be in and out of neighborhoods without anyone noticing that they had come or gone. That was before everyone had cameras everywhere. She glossed over the damage they did to those families, and felt less guilt, but that was later in their careers.

Early in life, their lives was hard on both of them, but he was there for her. Charlie was her saving grace. Somehow he was able to remind her that there was hope for a future without conflict, or at least they could pray about it. He prayed back then until he didn't.

Change comes quickly. She thought about how much both of them had grown as individuals. Charlie wanted to go back and live with his grandparents but was not allowed to see them. Once in a while they would show up at school just remind him that they had not forgotten about them. He would wave sadly but eventually ignored them.

Now it started to make sense. He use to talk about God much more as a ten-year-old. He remembered telling her about Jesus and how his sins were forgiven. He tried to lead her in a prayer of salvation, but she said no. She remembered how angry she got every time he would bring up God in all their conversations. She avoided him for a while. She could feel the anger coming back and overwhelming her soul. She looked again at her phone. She read the text once more: *Sleep well and say your prayers.* She threw her phone down on the ground. "He's one of them," she said and kicked it hard into her yard, only to go and retrieve it. *Or at least he's becoming one of them*, she thought. Her eyes filled with tears.

Chapter Five

....

Texas

One more morning; it was one more day. Pauline once again came downstairs after she had dressed and showered. Nothing on the agenda other than writing, and as before there was a morning knock. It was Charlie. She had not seen Charlie for a few weeks, but now he stopped by on a regular basis. He volunteered to do work for free, which initially she had rejected, but he had insisted on doing the work for free. It was a thank-you to her and secretly to his grandma.

He had tried not to think about it—that is, Grandma—and the fact that he was biding time until whatever Belmont was planning came out into the open. He hoped it would come out into the open. A verse popped into his head: "There is nothing concealed that will not be disclosed, and nothing hidden that will not be made known. What you have spoken in the dark will be heard in the daylight, and what you have whispered in the inner rooms will be proclaimed from the housetops" (Luke 12:2–3). He pondered and hoped God would make it true. He needed it for protection for her.

The preparation was impressive. He had paperwork where he had sketched out her entire yard. He showed where he wanted to plant old plants that she already possessed and put in new plants, some of which he dug up from his and Lucy's front yard. He wanted everything to look professional even if he had no expertise other than as a home gardener. He wore her down to acceptance.

The zero cost was what Pauline liked the best. She sipped her coffee in the morning and looked out her back window. She now admired the garden and yard. Surprisingly Charlie only asked for money for the material. Bert told her that under no circumstances was she to give him money. He said she would be "aiding and abetting" him for something that had not come to light. She laughed but agreed not to give him any money for anything other than materials.

It was a different story for Charlie. He had payment in his jacket pocket the night he met with Belmont. According to Belmont, he should have offered his services to Bert to throw off the scent. He did not care much about him or his advice. He only wanted to help Pauline because somehow he felt indebted to her.

Bert, none the wiser to anyone's motives, had every intention of asking for Charlie's help with his yard in the spring. He would also pay him even though he told Pauline not to give him money. After all, Charlie did not owe Bert anything yet.

It seemed to be a labor of love. Charlie said he was paying her back for taking him in that morning, and also she reminded him of his grandma, whom he dearly loved and missed. She felt the same, a debt and gratitude, as he labored for free, and she had no money to pay him. He had insisted working in the backyard only, since he was not sure of his ability. He often had another young woman with him, Lucy. Pauline liked both of them.

The gardening and arranging of the flowers was most impressive. The arrangement for the parts that were near the walkway and the house was done by Lucille. Lucy complained to Charlie at first, but only on the first day. Eventually she seemed to find sanctuary in not talking and just gardening, the same way as Pauline found solace in the springtime when she would plant her vegetables and fruits. She would show up sometimes without Charlie and ask to just hang out in the backyard, which was odd, but life can be odd sometimes. Pauline asked Lucy if she wanted to talk and come in for a while, but Lucy always said no, she had a mom. Uninvited, Pauline would come and sit beside her and talk with her. She was not sure about Lucille's comment but was not offended by it either.

The door was opened without the use of the intercom. The panicked expression was replaced by a simple smile. "Hey, Miss Pauline, can I use your bathroom?" Charlie said. "Then I am going to finish up in your backyard. I will be finishing up on the small bench. It's missing some slats, in the middle of the forest area where I blew the leaves. The gazebo on the left side of the house has the path swept clean as well as whitewash on the stone walkway leading to the swing within the gazebo. I also have some additions I want to show you how to work with your phone." Pauline was confused about additions but pointed to the bathroom anyway.

The bathroom was a small interior room, about the size of an elevator that was between the coat closet and the downstairs family room. It and the large pantry were used for shelter from tornados, since they had no windows and were in the middle of the house. Charlie exited and looked back at the bathroom. The bathroom had a fan that was barely running, and Charlie had forgotten to spray, Pauline presumed. "Is something wrong?" she asked. Charlie shook his head, but clearly there was.

The bathroom aligned with the pantry. Charlie looked around the corner. "Pantry?" asked Charlie. Pauline said it was. "I can have this redone as a panic room. The bathroom and pantry could be combined."

Pauline shook her head. It was unneeded. "No, I like it the way it is. Charlie, are you sure you are okay?"

They opened the back door onto the deck, and she was glad to be stepping outside. It was a beautiful morning, unseasonably warm, still fall but almost winter, and yet it felt like spring. "Sorry, Miss Pauline, I have taken my time with this. I wanted it to be done right," said Charlie.

She was not sure where he picked up the Miss Pauline instead of just Pauline, but she supposed it was just his way of paying her respect, or it had to do with his younger days with his grandparents.

The backyard was the best Pauline had seen. They walked down the steps and into the backyard. There were large white stones added to the surrounding of the flower bed. Perennials that bloomed in fall had been added above the brick wall that was behind the bushes. "I did not deserve any of this. And look, it is late in the season to be planting, but the plants still bloomed," said Pauline. There were other plants were dug up and replanted somewhere else in the yard. "It shaped up nicely compared to the little care it received." They returned to the deck area.

A black squirrel came and joined them from a few feet away on the deck. "It's God's grace," he said. "I have not been well since I met you, and it's affected Lucy too. At first she was terrified, but now she's a little off as well. It's like this: scripture keeps coming back to me, and I can't drown it out. I'm changing. I know it's true; that's not it, or maybe that *is* it. Maybe that's why it keeps coming back to me—because it's the truth." Pauline was quiet.

The squirrel was going back and forth on the rail of the deck. It then went up the lattice strung with juniper and back down and into the yard. They watched the squirrel in silence; then Pauline spoke. "I'm not sure what to do with that, other than to let you know that God's

Word is true and does not return void. If it had an impact on you when you were younger, and the Lord is bringing it back to you now, there is a reason. Do you know what it is?"

The outside brought Charlie freedom, and as the breeze came and went, he changed his mind. "No. I am going to try to finish up today if possible," he said. Pauline said it was fine. The conversation was over, or so she thought. She turned to walk away, but then there was a tap on her shoulder. Charlie had remembered something. Another verse came to his mind. "He who has been stealing must steal no longer, but must work, doing good with his own hands, that he may have something to share with the one in need," said Charlie. Pauline was puzzled.

Charlie's phone vibrated. It was Belmont, but he did not look. "That was well said," Pauline replied. She did not know he was just quoted scripture until she repeated it back in her head. "Oh, oh, oh, that is from the Lord, your verse," she said, a little taken aback. "To share with the one in need?" said Pauline who realized she was not supposed to be speaking at all.

The silence was unbearable for Pauline. She was not evangelical and did not know what to do with anything supernatural, but she believed in the power of the Holy Spirit. It was logical that God would give verses to verify and validate facts or other verses. "That one is new," said

Charlie. "I am not sure where I got it from, but it sticks with me. I wanted to move past it, but I couldn't. That was Ephesians 4:28. I don't say as many verses out loud anymore, but the verses are there. I also see verses now. If there is a verse anywhere, I am reading it.

"I accepted Jesus when I was younger and was taught by my grandparents about the Trinity, but I stopped living that life when I went to live with my mother. My grandparents died when I was in my teens, and I thought that part of me died with them. I know I can't be a Christian, not after all that I have done, but I am starving for God's Word—if that makes any sense."

It didn't. Pauline said, "I think you need to get baptized and talk to a pastor. Did you accept Jesus?" He nodded yes. "Then why are you taking the Christ out of Christian? The only thing that makes us Christians, and called by His name, is Christ Himself. Jesus died and rose again for our sins. Here's another one for you. It's from the New King James Versions. 'For You will not leave my soul in Sheol, nor allow Your Holy One to see corruption. It is also in the New Testament, in Acts 2:27. He is the God of the living. Our salvation is not in us but only in the risen Lord and Savior. 'Corruption' because the Holy One was rose on the third day. He did not undergo decay. We are in a process. We stand in the gap until we see Him face to face. It's about Him and what He did for us, not about us or what we do, other than believe. He just wants us to trust Him. He is the One who justifies us by faith in Him.", said Pauline.

Confidence can be a blessing. Charlie was now finding his footing. "Scripture doesn't lie as far as I am concerned. God does not reject a repentant heart. 'The sacrifice you desire is a broken spirit. You will not reject a broken and repentant heart, O God.' It's NIV version, Psalm 51, verse 17. The choice is to have faith in God and trust that He made a way for our sins to be forgiven and for us to be reconciled to Him for eternity through Jesus, the Son of God. That is what I believe and have chosen. It's as a clear as day to me. I'll meet with your pastor and be baptized right now.", said Charlie.

There were two bottles of water in the refrigerator. Pauline grabbed the waters and her purse, and they left for church. Charlie was baptized, but Pauline did not see him after that for a few weeks.

★★★

It's a date, was Pauline's only thought. Seth was at her door. He was a regular at church and he talked with her on the phone for at least fifteen minutes a few times a week. She was more excited about having a friend who was interested in her than she was about him, but she was willing to see where their friendship would lead.

The doorbell rang. She started to use the intercom

but then stopped. She invited him into her home. He went to kiss her on the cheek, and she pulled back. Weird but instinctual, she did not know him well enough for him to try to kiss her, even if it was only on her cheek. He looked just as he had on the day they went to get pizza, except for the material of the shirt. He wore a flannel plaid button-down shirt under his leather jacket. The shirt was untucked and hung over his blue jeans. She was not sure if that was a good look or not. It would blend in with everyone else in a shopping mall, she thought, although the malls were not as crowded as they used to be.

The coat closet was by the bathroom, under the staircase. She took his coat to put in the closet. "I can do that," he said and took his coat back. He looked at the bathroom beside the closet and told her that it would make a good panic room if there was ever a need. Pauline was starting to get a weird vibe. She could have Bert be the friend who interrupted the date if need be, but it was not planned.

Bert was staying home tonight and was aware that Pauline had plans but not that he would be a part of them. She looked at her phone, but there was no text from him, so he was probably streaming something on the TV. "What do we have on our agenda for this evening?" she asked. She usually had more control over her dates, but since this was their first and he had asked her out, she would let him choose. It was obvious he liked control.

The appetizers were on the cabinet, next to the unscented candles. Seth picked up the candles and looked at the bottom. "These are not scented. I can go either way depending what I am doing," he chuckled. "If I am taking a bath I might want to use a scented candle. As far as what our plans are, I thought I would let you choose. I was even thinking that we could stay in if you want. Maybe we could play cards in the sunroom."

The chills ran up Pauline's spine. *I did it again*, she chided herself. She had let a stranger into her house who clearly had issues. He must have been spying on her. He almost sounded as if he wanted to be Bert.

The weird feeling would go away as soon as the date was over, she told herself, just a few more hours. She opened the refrigerator and then the freezer. "I can find something for us to eat, I'm sure, and I love playing cards. How did you know?" She was going to ask what type of card games he liked to play, but if it was something odd, it would just add to her anxiety. "What did you think about church last Sunday?" she asked.

Bert had turned his phone to "do not disturb" around nine p.m., and it was now nine thirty. Pauline was not pleased. The only thing she had that was ready to eat was a vegetarian lasagna. It was a staple at her house, but she was getting tired of it. She went to warm the oven.

Seth picked up on her apprehension. He followed her and started to massage her neck, but she pulled away. "Sorry, you just seem so tight," he said. *What is with this woman?* he thought. "We can get a beer somewhere, unless you don't drink. I know this quaint place where you can watch a movie and order food. They also have a place to play pool."

Pauline exhaled. He was normal again. She just needed to set some boundaries. "I don't really know you that well, so if you don't mind not touching me." She did not want to sound like she was a prude, but she was for sure. "I am tight. It's been a lot of writing, and I spend my time sitting and not standing, so my neck and shoulders get the brunt of it." She was realizing how much she really did not like him.

The feeling was not mutual. "I thought you might want to stay home. I know that I do from time to time," said Seth. "Since you asked, I did like the sermon, especially the part about lambs among wolves."

She was being paranoid and making too big a deal out of nothing. She looked at her phone one last time; no text from Bert, and it was too late to call.

The frozen lasagna was on the cabinet beside the refrigerator. "That is good. It was Luke 10:3: *Go your ways: behold, I send you forth as lambs among wolves.* That's the verse, and God protects us." Pauline read the cooking instructions. The lasagna still frozen would take at least seventy minutes. "Maybe we could go out." She sent Bert a text that she was going out. He texted back the question, *who?* She told him who. He sent a text to *be careful*.

The lasagna package was still on the cabinet. He went to look at the package beside her. "This looks good, and it only takes seventy minutes to cook. So we have plenty of time to hang out. I need to call it an early night, not too early, but I need to be home by eleven," he said. Pauline was once again relieved.

The oven was almost preheated. She put the lasagna on a pan and stuck it in the oven. She asked what type of music he liked so she could play it on Alexa. He said he liked anything from the seventies, so she played seventies music from Alexa. "Have you been able to make any friends?" she asked.

She took out the ingredients to make a salad. He came and stood behind her. He placed his hand on her hips and started to dance. She did not turn around but rather walked away. "I have made one friend," said Seth and looked at her affectionately. She had no reply, and then he came closer to her. "Do I scare you? Do I make you feel uneasy?" he asked in a deeper voice. "I can go."

Creepy, she thought, but just then the lights in the backyard turned on, and she let that thought go. Her ADHD kicked in as she no longer heard the creepy way he asked his questions or the questions themselves. "Hey, look, I did not even know I had those lights. Those must be what Charlie did not finish explaining. I wonder if they are motion-sensing, but look at the pathways."

It was like staring at Christmas lights. Pauline stepped out of the kitchen and into the sunroom. "There are a lot of lights," Seth said. "I probably would not have put them so close together or so many in a row. I certainly would not have hung them on the outside of your sunroom."

There was no voice that she heard, especially not his. "Everything is lit up and so beautiful. Look at the lights showcasing the trees. Look what he did with the sunroom. It's perfect!" She raised her hands halfway as if she was worshipping and again was thankful. She walked out onto the deck and gazed at the sky. "There were no motion sensor lights on the deck, so they may not be working correctly. They should not be turned on right now if no one triggered them, get it? The rest must be on a timer. Perfect timing, wouldn't you say?" she said to Seth, who had followed her out on the deck. She walked back into the house.

The doorbell rang. Pauline rushed to see who it was. She did not hesitate to open the door and gave him a hug. "Oh, Charlie, thank you. I was just thinking about you. Did you do all those lights in the backyard?" She thought about it a little longer. "Did you just turn everything on, or is it on a timer?" Seth emerged from the kitchen to see who was at the door.

Charlie shut the door behind him. "Pauline, you know I did. I control it all from my phone. I wanted to show you that day but did not have a chance. I'll put it on your phone now and show you how it works if you have time. I also have a remote." He locked eyes with Seth. "You have company," he said. "I'm Charlie. I work with Pauline."

Pauline could not wait to find out what Charlie had installed. She texted Bert to come over and see the lights. She also texted him that she had lasagna and that Charlie had stopped by. *Bert, I hope you don't mind Charlie stopping by. I hardly see him and Lucy anymore.* She stopped texting and turned toward Charlie. "You have to stay for the lasagna. I just put it in the oven. Is Lucy in the car? Thank you again," she said and hugged him. She was normally not a hugger, but it was the culmination of the night that made him her new hero. Although Bert had only met him once, she was sure he would agree.

Bert texted Pauline back, *I am sticking unless you need me. Tell everyone hello. I have been playing phone tag with Seth. Tell him that we will get together sooner or later.*

The lights were too bright and could be seen from the hallway. Charlie held up the remote and dimmed the lights on the deck. "That is nifty, Champ," said Seth. "I'll take that from you, and you can go and check in tomorrow." Pauline was angry but tried to keep her cool.

The remote was tightly in Charlie's hand. "Nonsense," said Pauline. "He's part of the family." She turned to Charlie. "I don't know what I would do without you and Lucy." Charlie's smile was wide. "Now show me how this works. Too bad Lucy could not make it."

The lights were discreet. "I'm not surprised you didn't see them before now," said Charlie. "Now let me show you the neatest function for the lights: the color changes. The controllers even work with Alexa. I named the different lights differently. So for example, if you only want sunroom lights, those are the ones that are lit. Say dim and the lights will dim. Choose a color, and they will become that color. If you want all the lights to go on, then simply tell Alexa that you want to turn on all lights. They also had scenes for Christmas."

Seth was feeling left out and said that he would like to see it. He held out his hand for the remote, but Charlie just hit his group and Christmas scene on his phone. "I bet that was expensive," said Seth.

Charlie was trying hard to ignore him. The five thousand was in his pocket. "It was less than five thousand," he said. He looked at Pauline. "Just kidding, I had some of the items at home. It wasn't expensive." It started in the back of the yard and then the gazebo, and eventually all the lights turned to Christmas lights. It was not just green and red, but also smaller lights that were silver on the bottom that lit up.

He handed the remote to Pauline. "Aw, Charlie, it's beautiful," said Pauline. "You need to take a picture for Lucy or just bring her by here. You are staying for dinner?" He looked at Seth and said he would.

The lasagna finished baking, and everyone ate out in the sunroom under the Christmas lights. When eleven o'clock rolled around, Pauline reminded Seth that he had to leave. She wrapped some lasagna and salad for him and pushed him out the door. Charlie made up an excuse to walk him to the car.

Seth—Belmont—could not talk, he was so angry. He could not even threaten Charlie when he handed over the money. He drove away not letting his anger get the better of him.

The front of the house looked drab. Charlie figured he no longer needed to hang out in the back of the house since all bets were off with Belmont. "What if I do a little trim and lights to the front next week?" asked Charlie. Pauline said it was too much and she would insist on paying him. She had just received one of her first royalty checks for her last book. She went to her checkbook and wrote him a check for a thousand dollars, but he declined and quoted the same verse as before.

It took him another hour, but he finished setting everything up on her Alexa account and deregistered everything on his phone. "Hey, by the way, I am part of the pastor's small group now. I think he's taken a liking to me," said Charlie.

Pauline had never had children of her own, but felt Charlie was as close to a son as she could have. And although Charlie swore up and down that Lucy was no more than a friend, and she already had a mom, she was included too.

★★★

That night Belmont drove home only seeing red but had already devised a plan. Once again he was in front of his monitors. He watched Bert's house, but there was no activity other than one downstairs light being left on; all the other lights were shut off. Belmont decided he would go to bed, but before he did, he made one last phone call.

It was a long shot, but he was going to try. "Do you take side jobs?" Belmont asked. "I have resources who said I could contact you for a certain type of activity." His resources were real, but they had said that this guy was unreliable. However, that was not why Belmont chose him.

The voice was put on speaker. Stern put the phone next to him while he wrote down some information on a piece of paper. "I don't have to tell you that this call is confidential," Belmont said. "It pays five K, and if you are interested, I can meet you with more details." Stern agreed to meet him at a remote location.

Belmont hung up the phone satisfied. Now he would enact his revenge. He called Derby to coordinate the details. He looked at the picture of Pauline hanging next to his monitor. She'd had her chance, he said. He kissed his muscles attached to his biceps in self adoration. He had not quite decided what he would do with Pauline, but he had a few hours to think about it.

The sofa was already pulled out into a bed. He slept in the middle of the living room where he felt the most secure. He went to the bathroom to brush his teeth and washed up. He looked at his face and wondered when he had gotten so old. He thought he would have settled down by now. He looked at the picture of Pauline on his mirror, pulled it down, and dropped it in the trash.

Time to Spare

The itinerary of a mediocre writer was not as open as one would think, thought Pauline. She always seemed to be running out of time, even though she was not out and about like most authors. She had book signings; she just never left her kitchen table to sign them. Other than her daily errands, she needed to return a phone call to her editor and call her cousin back. Never a dull moment, she thought.

It had been a couple months since she had spoken to Sam. She had received several urgent voicemails within the last week, which she had been meaning to return. She had never gotten her invitation in the mail, so she figured Sam was calling to officially invite her. She had wished she had a definite plus-one, but she was still on the fence about who she might ask.

She was still moving at a snail's pace when it came to writing the novel. She had switched back to the computer from the typewriter and then back to the typewriter. She would stick it out with the typewriter. She did make the concession of an outline.

The laptop that laid on the kitchen counter was now what she coveted. *Come play a game*, she could hear it whisper, or *Don't you need to check your email?* In the end, it prompted, *What about your finances? Did you receive that payment you were waiting for?* No, she thought, the typewriter was the perfect writing tool, but for some reason no matter what device she used to write the novel, it was slow going.

Praise and worship was not so bad for a topic. The character, Kara, was three chapters into her post apocalyptic world. Her country had changed from one of freedom of religion to one where no one worshipped or praised anything of religious value. The marketplace had changed too. It was hard to find work or food. Many of her friends were leaving the country, but she chose to stay. She had a better understanding of her purpose. She needed to stay.

It was praise and worship that grounded Kara during the growing darkness. She had come to know her God as the Christian God who would meet all her needs. In Him she would have to trust for the good, the bad, and the ugly, and she had seen her fair share of ugly. The praise and the worship kept her doing just that.

Pauline continued to write.

> Kara once again looked to the left and to the right before approaching the narrow entrance to the building. She went down the path to the brick wall. There she crouched down and found a small clay jar. She quickly retrieved the key and entered the room that had been prepared for them. There she saw several women like herself with no place to worship or to praise except the confines of the four walls that surrounded them. Someone brought wine and bread for communion; then they would start their meeting with prayer and a small something to eat. Everyone there was delighted to see the other joyful faces. Their group got smaller at times, but mostly because they would seek safe haven somewhere else.

The phone was on "do not disturb," but somehow it disturbed. Pauline continue to write despite the attention-seeking summons to a video chat. *What is it? Why can't I get quiet? I live by myself for heaven's sakes—no dog, not even a goldfish, just the way I like it.* She turned over the phone, and it was Sam. She was placing a video call. "Hey, Sam, how are you?" She tried not to sound irritated or agitated, but it was hard not to be.

The ceiling looked like any other outdated office ceiling. It had big squares that were connected by little strips of thin metal. Pauline immediately put down her phone too. She wanted to place it up staring at something rotten, but it was too much effort. She began to review and proof her story so her time would not be a complete waste.

Unable to concentrate, she was glad when Samantha finally spoke. "Fun fact," she said as Pauline typed furiously. "If you use the video function with just audio and your phone is on 'do not disturb,' then the 'do not disturb' works, but if you use the video for a video chat, it voids out the 'do not disturb' or 'no notifications.' That is how I got in touch with you! You phone rings incisively until you pick it up. Get it?" Sam paused, but Pauline continued to type. "I assume you had your phone on 'do not disturb.' Can you pick up your phone? I can only see the cobweb on your fan? Is that a kitchen fan?" she said. She took a screenshot of it so she could look at it more closely later. "You need to dust especially, if that is over your—"

Pauline picked the phone up to see Sam's face much too close. The video chat function of the phone was lost on Pauline. Her publisher insisted that she and a few other authors had a zoom conference call once a month. It was her publisher's brainstorm of an idea that everyone could collaborate on their stories for better content. As it was, most authors were leery of sharing their ideas other than with those they chose. She really wanted to just hold the phone to her ear or put in her Bluetooth earbuds. "Any chance you can call me back, and we can have a normal conversation?" asked Pauline. "I'll answer it when you call me back instead of letting it go to voicemail." Sam agreed.

The second cup of coffee was in the works when Samantha eventually called Pauline back. "Hey again, sorry about that," Sam said. "I got hung up. I remember why I wanted to video chat with you besides just getting my call to go through to you. I wanted to ask you something very important and see your reaction when I ask you. Can we try the video chat again?"

The supplemental cup of coffee to her daily routine was French roast. It would get her through the rest of the morning. She had put in her earbuds and was at peace holding her cup of Joe with both hands. "No," said Pauline. Sam threatened to stop by in person, but Pauline said she would make a point of not being there. "Is it the same as before, you want me to just come to the church and not the reception? I'll be okay Fine!" she said, disappointed.

The coffeepot would not be upgraded since the sale of her last book was not as good as she had expected. The current book, still in its first print, was promising. She wondered when things would be better. It could be worse. "No, I am not at that stage yet. I do have your invite done with a plus-one, because you are special, but everyone else's is being done by my matron of honor, Pauly!" She paused. "That's not why I'm calling. I want you to be one of my bridesmaids. In fact, I want *you* to be my matron of honor, if you choose to accept. Please say yes. I am so excited, you don't know. It never even occurred to me to ask you."

Had anything been in Pauline's mouth she would have spit it out. "What happened to your matron of honor?" asked Pauline. Before she made up an excuse as to why she would not be able to be her matron of honor, she figured she needed to hear Sam out.

The cousin situation had always been pushed to the limit but this was to the brink of the brim. "Some best friend, right?" said Sam. "We'd been friends for a little over a year. I met Mia when I first moved here. We hit it off. She even invited me to a Bible study at her house. I almost went! She really is a nice person, and kind. After all, kindness is what really matters, and she apologized. She said she had family situations she needed to attend to."

Pauline was quiet. "That's tough," she said. They both understood family was important. Family always came first. "So you are it, Pauly. Would you please accept?" said Sam, pausing before she went on, "I already put your invite in the mail with a plus-one, just in case that ever happens for you."

The coffee cup she loved the most was in her hands. It was a prayer for strength. "I need a little while to think about it," said Pauline. "You might want to think of someone younger."

The picture that Sam had in her hands of her and Pauline as kids showed Pauline as a tall lanky girl and Sam, shorter by seven inches and younger by seven years. "I already thought about that. I have someone who does fantastic makeup. You won't even look like yourself," said Sam. She snapped the picture with her phone and sent it via text to Pauline.

The picture was of a different time and a different era. Pauline deliberated before she uttered her next word. "Sure. Unless Mia's schedule frees up, in which case you should go with her as your matron of honor. I am going to need a lot of information from you—and Mia's number." She was already formulating a plan to get Mia back into the wedding party, front and center.

Sam picked up the picture and kissed Pauline. "Sure," she said. "I have to go, but thank you for saying yes. It will be great! Oh, and I am pretty sure Mia is moving out of the country."

★★★

Promotions and transfers were on the rise. Many officers were transferring to other divisions, while others were just quitting. Jay and Bert enjoyed working together even if everything was getting a little tougher for them. Captain Jaks was no longer gracious about lending Bert to the FBI and the detective squad. He wanted him back on the beat.

Bert did miss the beat of the street. On the other hand, he liked being a detective, although he would hardly admit it. He had purpose again, not only to arrest but to find. Not only did they toil over their initial interdepartmental case for which he was requisitioned, but several cases came out successfully in a couple of months. The most recent case was a homicide. It was the most disconcerting for Bert as it involved Charlie.

The jerky was "buck" jerky. It was homemade by Bert. Bert seasoned, dried, and froze it. It was a Nugent recipe handed down from his mom, a big fan. They sat chewing on jerky and searching the pictures of the crime scene for clues. "It's disturbing," said Bert. Jay agreed but was glad that they had the culprit in custody. Bert was not so sure. "I don't think so."

They were almost always on the same page, except for now. Jay said, "If this is one of your gut instincts, I would have to disagree. I think it's obvious that Charlie crossed someone and was either defending himself or this was an out-and-out premeditated murder. Any judge would convict on just the evidence."

Bert pushed the pictures aside. "It's not right. Let's go over everything." They talked about motive, opportunity, and means. It feels contrived. Everything is too neat and tidy.

The disinfectant wipes were on the table with the photographs. Every time either of them picked up a photograph, Jay would wipe the table as if they were cleaning up the crime scene. Bert caught on and pointed it out. Jay was still getting used to being a detective, which psychologically at times was hard to handle. He wished it was only so easy for things to be clean. He looked again at the whiteboard. "The only thing we really don't have is admission of guilt," he said.

That might be, thought Bert. "I'm not saying Charlie shouldn't be sitting in jail. He's done his fair share of crimes, but this does not speak of rage but derangement. This is much too tidy and set up. The profiler said it was serial." The profiler input was a weak link, and Bert knew it. They would have to come up with evidence to the contrary, not just testimony, if they did not want to convict Charlie.

Normally, he would not have gone with his hunch, even if it was right, when the evidence was so damning. He would have talked himself out of the suspect's innocence and washed his hands of it. His logic was that he would be guilty of something, but as a detective it was on him to get the right person. This was no different; he had met Charlie and knew firsthand that this act was not him.

The pictures were gathered once again. Jay sat

thumbing through the photos. "You might be right, way too professional. We got to get this guy. Everything about this is wrong. Charlie can stay put for a while here at the station. I'll put in the request that he does not get transferred."

Bert had observed that Jay was better as a detective than a cop. Jay's background was military intelligence. Bert never asked him why he transitioned, but it may have had something to do with his dad being a cop. "We are the big fish in the little pond, now.", Jay said, jokingly. "I'll try not to let it go to my head and stay humble. We are making a difference," he added, and Bert agreed.

Detective Captain Murphy came in and requested their presence. The office door closed, and the blinds were shut. Murphy asked for a quick update on their cases, specifically the classified case in which they were working with the agency.

The Nespresso machine had a waiting line. It was DC Murphy, Bert's nickname for the Captain, Bert, and then Jay was last in line. DC looked over his shoulder. "You guys okay with moving floors? We are opening a new division for collaborating departments and agencies. We have special funding. With everything being defunded, refunded, and now funded, they have sanctioned a special workforce. Everyone is scratching their heads as to how things have gone in a straight decline. Crime is at a new all-time high, up by over 50 percent in the last year. That is with lumping together homicides, which is higher than 50 percent, with every other type of crime."

The Nespresso machine was out of water. Bert opened the water bottle beside it and filled the coffee machine. It was not protocol to use water bottles to refill the water bin since it was too much plastic, but no one said anything. "The state and cities are in denial," said Bert, "but the federal government has to do something without summoning the National Guard. It's the wild, wild west. It comes down to funding localized militias and enacting martial law. It's not just corruptible but is in most cases giving criminals guns, even with proper vetting. We, as officers of the law, have to go through extensive two-year training. I am not sure if that is every state. To whom are they accountable, and what qualifications do they have? Lastly, they will be paid twice as much as a street cop. So one of them is better than two of us. Bert made two cups and handed one to Jay.

The window overlooked the parking lot. They stood looking down at the street. Bert went on, "That's why the government is investigating this organization which is petitioning for funding and at the same time is funding legislation in all states requiring that the state and local enforcement agencies be dismantled with no more funding. The lobbyists on the Hill represent many organizations, but the request for funding goes back to a few sources. This particular source has ties internationally into criminal activity and has been linked to several murders of government officials."

Eventually Bert and Jay moved to their chairs in front of DC's desk, where he was now standing, though neither sat. DC continued where he left off. "There is funding for our office to be working with the federal government. Your specific case falls under that; as for the other cases, let me just thank you." Jay and Bert smiled. Bert stared downward, as usual.

High-fives were off the table, too somber of a moment. They both were still enamored with new jobs, especially Jay. He wanted to say something along the lines of a good Western, *"No need for thanks, we're just doing our job."* He envisioned himself hitting himself on his butt and galloping around the room. He chuckled to himself. "Thank you for making this possible," said Jay in the end.

They missed the streets, but the criminals that they were catching on the street were a trickle-down effect. Getting people to care about their own communities and report each other was a talent, Jay thought. Bert would say it came with prayer.

The institution was changing, but so was the government, along with the criminals and the American people as a result. "It's more than a cross-fit program," said DC. "It could start a merge if local and state governments start falling under anarchy. A floor is being dedicated as classified. Some of us are working to get more officers classified, depending on their backgrounds, which also helps with the vetting that our state and local governments are requiring of all police officers. Mind you, that is not the clearances they require but the vetting to prevent police brutality and incompetence." He tried to be matter-of-fact, but thought the process was counterintuitive, targeting not the issue but the officer.

The topic was hard to discuss. "It almost seems surreal," said Jay, "and it's why most officers are quitting. Not just because of the pay scale or lack of respect and discrimination, but because they are targets physically and socially. It's why I was looking for a safer area for me and my family. No one ever thought it would go back to the days when the badge would be pinned on whoever was the most courageous and was willing to get shot first." It made for a good cowboy movie, but not so entertaining when it came to real life, Jay thought.

The information that they had could not be laid out, as it was in a locked safe. It would be good to have a floor that was dedicated to security. It would be easier. "So that is our update. When will this take place?" asked Bert. DC told them to follow as he led them to the secured floor which now held their offices.

★★★

The police had Charlie, and the group was divided. Lucy knew it would be her only time to leave. She wanted to wait it out for Charlie, but she knew she had to get out of there before she got in too deep.

Stern was quick to take control. He made offhanded remarks about drugs and women and how lucrative the business was. She studied Treble, a follower, but whose follower? She had never seen him as person before now. She wondered if he would be better off going with her or rotting with Stern.

The den was diminished without Charlie. Lucy tried to remain cool, but she knew she had no backing without him. The meeting started with Stern making some offhanded remarks about Lucy. Treble laughed. Treble looked her up and down which he had never done before this meeting. *Okay, Treble,* she thought to herself, *it was nice knowing you. I'm out of here.* She wanted to torch the place. She never realized that Charlie was the balance to their group of cat burglars. It was clear now that he was why she'd stayed and was now her reason for leaving.

It was on the way to her connecting flight, from Salt Lake City to Dallas Fort Worth, where he caught up to her. "Did you drop this?" asked Belmont. Lucy looked at what he handed her and then at him. She could get out of this, but how? She did not know for sure it was him, but she knew that it would not take long for him to give himself away. Charlie had described him to down to every last detail. So far same build, but it would be his mannerisms that would give him away. The condescension in his voice. She handed it back to him and said it wasn't hers.

It was an iPhone cord with an adapter. It looked like hers, but she was not going to check. She traveled with two, and one was in her overhead luggage. "I have to catch my next flight," she said. She continued to her gate and he followed. It had to be him. She was not sure how she would lose him. She did not have to get on the flight.

The restroom was to her right. She never let on that she knew he was behind her, but her phone acted as a mirror. She ducked in the restroom and then one of the stalls. She had to think of something. She was not tied to any mode of transportation. Her father was a cop. She would just explain the whole thing when she got home to Fort Worth, and he should be able to help her, but she had to make it home.

She exited the stall with her luggage. "I just want to get home, please, Lord," she said. An African American woman heard her say something ending with "please, Lord." She put her hand over her shoulder but did not touch her and repeated the two words. They parted ways, and Lucy exited the restroom, looking back. That was weird.

There was no one around. She looked in her purse. "Son of a bitch," she exclaimed. It was her iPhone cord and adapter that were missing. How the hell did he get a hold of it? She knew it was Belmont. She looked around for him and could not see him anywhere.

It was Belmont's voice that stayed in her head. "I know you set Charlie up, you son of a bitch," she whispered as she bent to retrieve her other adapter from the front pocket of her luggage. She pulled the cord from the pocket and started walking.

The gate was further down. She placed the cord in her purse, and as she checked for her gate, she felt something touch her shoulder. "Lucy?" he said. She turned around and took the palm of her hand and went for his chin, but he caught her hand and almost tripped her. She swung her leg around and found her balance. She immediately went for his groin with her knee, but he was too quick.

She started to focus. "FBI," said the agent standing next to Bert. He showed her his badge, which identified him as Agent Dinwiddie. "We would like you to come with us. We should have you home before dinner with time to spare."

★★★

Gate 44 was just ahead; Belmont would have time to spare. He canceled his flight to Fort Worth. He saw the agents in time and went in the other direction. His next flight, to a small island in the South Pacific, was soon to board. He waited in his tropical button-down shirt and khaki shorts.

Chapter Six

Change

The top floor was under renovation. Everything was being moved around and to other floors. Bert and Jay took up a small corner of the floor. "Hey," said Jay, jabbing Bert in the ribs. "This is exciting, yes?" Bert was silent. They worked, temporarily, in a large corner office which eventually would house some VIP, but for now they had dibs. Contractors were coming and going, making adjustments to everything. This project not only had funding but the expense of securing the building must have cost a fortune, Bert figured.

The office windows were being taken out and replaced with shatterproof glass. The landlines were not those of the old days. The classified communications that would be in a SCIF, a Sensitive Compartmented Information Facility, with actual turn-key technology. "So all of this is newer technology?" asked Bert.

Jay knew more about the old technology and the new technology than Bert. He explained to Bert a lot of cutting-edge information of which Bert had never heard. Along with Detective Captain Murphy, they were also being briefed daily on classified technology as well as information. "It's the newest from my understanding," said Jay.

The professionalism of their white-collar environment was at another level compared to the police department, which was very bureaucratic and did not lack protocol. What it lacked was intimate knowledge that brought respect for each other's position. Bert never knew a job could be so fun. He had autonomy and purpose. He tried to remain humble so not to lose his edge and be caught up in the job and not its function.

Detective Captain Murphy had another briefing scheduled. They were making progress on the case originally assigned to them. All notes and documents were still locked up, as the top floor was still not finished. But their minds were sharp, and they were ready to share where they were with Belmont and others.

The elevator door opened, and out stepped Detective Captain Murphy. He held a box that was heavy and wide. Jay offered to help him with it, but he declined. Bert opened the door to the conference room.

Detective Captain Murphy was all smiles. "Hey, look at this." he said and started to open the brown industrial box and then stopped. He picked up the phone in the conference room and dialed 9. "It's here. Yes, in the conference room, top floor." Less than a minute later the elevator doors opened, and two men stepped out.

They came to the conference room, and Captain Murphy pointed to the box. They opened the box and inspected and scanned the pieces for any electronic components that were out of place, the way security would do at the airport. "Are you sure you don't mind doing this?" asked Detective Captain Murphy. After giving the coffee machine the thumbs-up, they started to assemble the commercial espresso/coffee machine.

There was a small stand behind the conference table where the espresso machine was placed. Murphy pulled a bag of thermal coffee cups from his briefcase. He then pulled a grocery sack from the same briefcase that contained a small container of milk and sugar. "DC, you are the captain," said Jay. Jay noticed that there was no water for the coffee machine. He nudged Bert again. They both had unopened water bottles with them as well as the ones they were drinking. They poured the water from the bottles into the coffee machine.

Once again, they lined up. The new conference room was bare, but no one minded. "You've made fantastic progress," said "What type of news do you want first, great, good or bad?"

It was rhetorical. Jay shrugged. "The good news would be fine," said Bert.

Detective Captain Murphy was in a great mood. "I'll give it to you straight," he said. "Lucy, as you know, would not have been able to be apprehended at Fort

Worth had no FBI or military jurisdiction been allowed without her being brought back here and involving other Fort Worth police. Our team will have more leverage for the state to move quicker or more efficiently than in the past; local goes global. What is your take, Bert, from this case file?"

It was implied to Bert and Jay that a team was being assembled. It was above their pay grade, but military, agency, and local enforcement could be the new adjustment that would not only police the streets but follow the money to greater sources of crime.

They all had coffee in hand. It was the little things that made life great. "It's working," said Bert. "We were able to question Lucy and secure detail for her at home in Fort Worth. She is willing to testify against the person known as Belmont if we ever catch him, now that his cover is blown. Although she had never seen him, Charlie, who is in our custody now for a homicide, has. She was only aware of the one meeting that Charlie had with Belmont. He has not been identified yet in the FBI database."

The good news came first. "It's Lucy that ties everything together, and with Charlie's testimony, we will be able to get him. There are connections to Belmont and the homicide for which Charlie has been incarcerated without bond. Charlie will be released soon, but we may be able to drum up some other charges to keep him in custody, for his own safety."

Jay nodded. "I put in a 'no transfer' request for him that was granted. He can stay with me after he gets out. I have a condo that I rent out on Sixth Street that I can use." The lack of protocol of the new organization let them bend the rules.

Detective Captain Murphy liked his two-man team and was proud of their work. "Two local suspects have also been picked up and booked. Their testimony also points to Belmont and one other person who is off the grid. No one has ever seen him or knows of his existence, but his fingerprints showed up at 'the den' on a detonation device and matched fingerprints at the murder scene. We are running the fingerprints against the FBI's database but do not expect anything to turn up. Both these guys are big-money hired assassins posing as normal people to gain access to information."

Bert and Jay laughed. "That is a stretch, but okay," said Jay. "Did you have any other information?" They were in over their heads, and espionage was far-fetched. Bert quieted; it rang true as he thought about the deer in his backyard and two different entities involved.

There it was, the green on the team—lack of experience. "Yes, I will get to it. The confession of a Treble Clark and a Stern Regard have almost exonerated Charlie, incriminated themselves and our mystery villain Belmont. Treble and Stern were lucky to have us pick them up, too, as 'the den' was wired to blow; we found the detonation device," said Detective Captain Murphy. He stopped and walked back to the coffee machine and patted it on the top. "I would have never got funding for this baby."

Both Bert and Jay felt a bit uneasy. "Picked up too? You'll get to that later?" asked Jay. The captain nodded. "So that was the great news?" said Jay. Bert was looking down as he always did when he was contemplative. One thing he hated most about being a cop was that he felt like he stood alone, but there was hope on the horizon.

It was Bert's turn to refill his coffee cup. "Yes," said the captain, "it's a lot of information, but you will be caught up after this. The great news is the good and the bad together. The bad news is that Belmont was at the airport, but we found out too late. We caught him on camera, so we have some idea what he looks like, but it gets better. Lucy was picked up at the right time. She was not sure, but she thought he was there at the airport stalking her. He probably assumed she never made that connection to him or he would not have gotten on another flight. The great news is this: the island to which he traveled was for another hit. The man, Rick Slight, was subpoenaed over two years ago to testify against—get this—one of the sources who could be responsible for funding this terrorist organization."

Jay was holding his second cup of coffee and watching the workings come and go. They made a substantial amount of progress in a short time. "And?" asked Jay. He was starting to feel a little lost.

Detective Captain Murphy decided to stand too. "Things have come together in not much time. He is willing to testify to what he knows. He even will take a chance on the witness relocation program," said DC. "So on to the next topic of business. Although you would not make the cut, the department wants you to have an abbreviated version of training as field operatives."

Bert and Jay looked at each other with dismay. "Haven't we been thrown into the fire already?" Bert asked. "Is it necessary? We were cops." He briefly wished he was back on the street. "I liked being a cop. You just went and got the bad guy, and I was good at it."

DC circled the table, not sure what else to say, but it was a matter of need-to-know. "Bert, don't ask me how I know, but you were on that list—the list of people they needed to have knocked off. You are good at it, and now you are better at this. You both close twice as many investigations with solid evidence than my most seasoned detectives. This team is for you. You and Jay give a damn; maybe that's what it takes." Then the DC added, "So what if you both may need to lose a little weight and gain a little muscle and dexterity?"

No one laughed. "I squeeze in my morning run," said Jay. "I guess it would be kind of cool to know what they know for conversation's sake."

The floor had cleared. "It's getting close to lunchtime," said the DC. "I just want to remind you about what we're trying to accomplish." He went to the whiteboard and started to draw the different organizations, what they did, and how they corresponded with operations.

Bert and Jay left for lunch. They discussed what they saw as cops and how it had changed in the last decade.

The pizza place that neither of them had tried was across the street. "Game?" asked Bert. Jay nodded. "On an individual scale, it's hard to see what is happening to Americans as they are becoming more drug dependent, less self-sufficient, and not accountable to any federal authority. Think about the last time we pulled over a car and it did not have drugs in it."

Jay nodded in agreement. "It has changed since, even within the last decade. People steal for drugs, they drive with drugs in their system, and they die on drugs. The saddest thing is that they get involved with drugs one small, bad choice at a time. When we were in school they had films we had to watch for a whole as part of our physical education that showed the effects of drugs. All the movies basically ended with 'Just say no,' like most of the commercials. Most of us were too scared to try drugs, except for hemp. We knew that our brains looked like eggs in a frying pan after doing drugs. And the drugs now are worse."

The topic was starting to draw attention from some of the locals who were in the restaurant. Someone sitting nearby chimed in: "People can move to some state, Oregon or California, a state that would hold them less accountable for crimes like drugs, lack of citizenship or criminal protests, threatening officials and vandalism."

The man was eating a slice of pizza and a beer and raised his pizza. They must have been talking too loudly. "Is that the answer? Is there nothing that can be classified as a true crime other than homicide?" asked Bert. The man said no with a mouth full of pizza and went back to his meal. They realized they might have been talking a little too loudly, but they were on their way out.

Once out on the sidewalk Bert started to talk about the new agency. "If the crime took place in a state with federal legislation for this new organization, they would be able to pursue warrants and gain information. The intel would not be lost crossing state lines, whether minor or of a much larger scale. It could be investigated and prosecuted quicker and with closure. Also, officers would be safer if they had other backing from the federal government, especially in cases of anarchy. It seems like a win–win for every state."

The truth was out there. Jay was starting to see it. He stayed away from politics but found the opposite was true, too. "I can see that. I get what you are saying about true crimes, but it can also be said for individual rights as well. Certain constitutional freedoms of citizens should not wane from state to state. To bear arms, form militias, and defend themselves, to worship as they please and to speak freely without censorship should be rights for every American no matter what state they live in or what venue they choose to express their opinion. There is hope for America and the individual, united on their fundamental, unalienable rights under God as citizens. Those rights should not be scattered depending on what state a person resides." Jay chuckled. "Instead of the United States, America should be called the Federated Republic or the Not United United States, the NUUS."

Bert laughed. Jay always had a way of bringing humor into everything. They went their opposite ways. Jay did not double back as he had when he worked under Captain Jaks. This job was a better fit for both of them.

Bert thought about it later on the way home. There had to be light at the end of the tunnel while the crime rates soared to epic levels and state and local governments tried to sort through the logistics of law enforcement. There must be hope, not in change and not in complacency, but in caring enough to go forward. They found a way in their state to go forward in unification against the destruction, theft, and murder that were robbing a nation of its morality. The mob mentality that was stealing wanted "what was theirs" as people thought more about what they did not have instead of what they had. On a general level, they wanted everyone to be the same; that seemed fair, but fair is not just or righteous. It is just accountability on a horizontal level that took God and capitalism out of the equation.

If a nation could humble themselves, perhaps a tunnel could be built with His blessing as He would make a way even in the midst of dissension. While the dichotomy between the haves and the have-nots multiplies, and hearts turn away from God, people pray. Their government was doing something to maintain order during the civil unrest. God has the absolute authority, for all authority is from above, and perhaps He will bless it.

Bert could be more thankful for what he had and especially for the right to have. He was thankful for his position within the department, even if the department was only comprised of a few other people. He was thankful for Jay and DC. The captain had perhaps saved not only his life but those of the future recruits from other departments. Civil unrest was the number-one concern of the nation, and it was affecting all of law enforcement.

★★★

The classroom was enormous. Pauline entered the church and waited outside the classroom for Mia, but one of the children told on Pauline. "There is an adult waiting outside of the classroom for you. I asked her who she's waiting to see, and she said Mia. I said I would get you, but she said she would just wait," said Gabrielle. Mia laughed as she walked toward the door.

The door was already open so she just popped her head out to see around the corner. "Let me guess—Pauline? You came early. Come on in, unless you are afraid of children.", she said and paused. She made a scary face at her nine- and ten-year-olds. "Do you have a scary face?" she asked the class. As Pauline joined the classroom, the children made their best attempts at scary faces. Some children even growled.

The classroom had other children with other teachers in different corners of the room. There were also cameras in the corners of the classroom. Pauline did not know how she felt being on camera but took a seat catty-corner from where Mia stood. "Thank you for letting me join," she said. Pauline was not afraid of a little Sunday school, though she never volunteered at her own church.

The scales of justice were placed in the middle of their circle. They discussed what was fair and what was not. Mia then used the example of Job to show that God's justice is better than what is fair. God brought what was just to all of mankind by way of a sacrifice, but not what was fair. "By all fairness, what should we get if we cause trouble?" Mia asked.

The boys sat quietly together. George raised his hand. "When I cause trouble, I get punished," he said. The other boys looked at each other and nodded in agreement.

Pauline said that was a good answer. Mia ignored Pauline and addressed the class. "If we all deserve punishment no matter how good we try to be, since the Lord says even to call someone a fool is so sinful to Him that it deserves hellfire, what would you ask God to do? We all deserve punishment."

All young ladies' hands shot up. Clever girls, always having an answer, when no one else did. It was the age. It lasted up until junior high. "It's Jesus," said Gabby. "He made the way. He took our punishment upon Himself so we would not get punished because of our sinfulness."

So true, Mia thought. "Anyone else?" she asked. Josie raised her hand. *This is going to be good*, thought Mia. Jo had the most delightful and interesting way of looking at things.

"The punishment is death," said Josie. "As soon as Eve ate the apple, she sinned because she disobeyed. But if she hadn't, would we still have Jesus?" She knew the teacher was getting ready to cut her off, so she quickly added what she really wanted to say. "Jesus saved us from death eternally and hellfire. He was our sacrifice for our sin, so whatever sin we do that separates us from God's holiness, our debt would be paid if we accept the Son of God as our Savior.

It goes like this: John 3:16—'For God so loved the world, that He gave His only begotten Son, that whosoever believes in Him should not perish but have everlasting life.'"

Mia was taken by Jo's answer. She had great understanding. Mia said, "Scripture says, in John 1, verses 2 and 3, 'He was in the beginning with God. All things were made through Him, and without Him nothing was made that was made.' Did that answer your question?"

Jo nodded yes. So Mia continued. "Those were great answers. So fair in the case of sin is punishment, but what is just and righteous comes from God. Perfect love casts out fear because fear involves punishment—also in scripture. So what we think is fair is not always just or right, so sometimes we have to go back to God and trust Him for what is right. Sometimes it requires patience." She still ignored Pauline who was truly enjoying her visit.

She continued with the story of Job and quoted scripture, from Job 1:9–12. "So Satan answered the Lord and said, 'Does Job fear God for nothing? Have You not made a hedge around him, around his household, and around all that he has on every side? You have blessed the work of his hands, and his possessions have increased in the land. But now, stretch out Your hand and touch all that he has, and he will surely curse You to Your face!' And the Lord said to Satan, 'Behold, all that he has is in your power; only do not lay a hand on his person.'"

The boys' hands shot up. There were a couple of questions at once. "So the devil was not allowed to kill him?" asked John. Another boy, Jim, answered and said no, the devil could not kill him, but he was able to do evil to him. Jim answered the following question as well.

Mia nodded her head in agreement with his answers. "The devil wants none to have redemption. He wanted punishment for all. It is why the devil enticed Eve in the first place and why he was allowed to afflict Job, but Job also believed in what was just and trusted in God for his circumstances. Job had scabs with worms, his family and wealth were destroyed, and his precious faith was shaken, but even through his days of grumbling he held to his promise of his Redeemer. It's in chapter 19, verses 25 and 26, NIV version: 'I know that my Redeemer lives, and that in the end He will stand on the earth. And after my skin has been destroyed, yet in my flesh I will see God." said Mia in conclusion—or so she thought.

One hand shot up. "So even though Jesus had not been born yet, Job still believed that Jesus was his hope for redemption and that he would be justified by his faith in Him?" asked Jo. *Wow*, Mia thought and told her yes. "Interesting," Jo said.

Mia was amazed and excited at their understanding, which had begun with the teaching of the knowledge of the Holy One. "Love found a way. It was just but not fair.", said Mia. It was time to go.

The class stood up, and they did not have to wait like the younger ones for their parents to come and get them. "Thank God for that, just but not fair." said Gabrielle putting her hand to her forehead. Jo shook her head up and down with her eyes wide open.

The classroom emptied, and Pauline and Mia straightened it up before leaving for lunch. They discussed Sammie's wedding. Mia agreed to be her matron of honor, while Pauline was Sammie's first point of contact for everything. Pauline would handle the bridal shower and coordinate the dress fittings for the wedding party. She also consented to doing anything else that needed to be done, but it still would be Mia who was the proxy-lead. Mia thanked Pauline for her understanding. Pauline was grateful in return.

★★★

It was his turn. Pascal had done everything to get what he had done out of his head. His aim was true, and his thoughts were justified, but then why the guilt of what he had done? It was tremendously heavy, and yet he knew it was no big deal.

Why me? Those he hung around with in college were loyal to the same causes and participated in the same protests he had, so where was their guilt. It was not fair that he had to be the one with a conscience.

Pascal took the pair of kicks from his closet that still had the price tag on it and slid it into a brown paper bag from the local grocery store. He looked at his shoes and shook his head. He got into his car and drove to Brooker's.

He had walked by the store a thousand times since he had robbed it. He was there when the front window was broken. He was there when it was repaired. He was there when business started coming back. His friends told him that insurance covered everything, including the merchandise stolen, but still …. He looked at the brown bag that he carried in his hand.

Brooker's was front and center. He parked on the street in front of the store. He got out. He had a bad feeling about it as the cars whizzed by him. He took the handwritten note from his pocket and placed it in the bag. He put it in the doorway, but an old man was entering the store, so he picked it back up. He held the door as the man entered.

The bag was held in his hand. "Is that lunch?" the old man asked. He was not sure about how delivery was done these days. "If so, I'll take it," he said. "I work here."

Pascal's grip on the bag tightened. "I'm not sure," he said. He relinquished the bag. The man looked inside of the bag. He looked back at Pascal confused. "I'm returning them for a friend." The man took out the note and read it.

The note was then folded back into a square and put back into the bag. "This isn't a return; this is a confession.", said the old man sternly. "I think you need to come in for a minute while I call the police. Is that your car?"

The car was double-parked, front and center, underneath the corner camera. Pascal nodded yes, and his eyes welled up with tears. "Mercy," said Pascal. "I truly am sorry and was trying to do the right thing. God was telling me I needed to return them to you."

The man looked at the bag and then at Pascal. "I don't believe in God. Come inside, and we'll see if we can't sort this out with the police. My name is Mr. Kower, and I'm the owner; just your luck."

Pascal muttered a cuss word, which he wished he could take back since it seemed to delight Mr. Kower. The door was held open for Pascal, but Pascal shook his head no. "I'm not going anywhere, but I'll wait out here if it's all the same to you." Mr. Kower pointed to the camera and said his license plate out loud in Pascal's hearing. He said his memory was still as sharp as ever.

The store was operating as usual. The friendly young man who greeted everyone who entered the store was waiting for Mr. Kower to step inside. "Greetings, Mr. Kower. How was your morning?" asked Kao. The older man responded with a hand up in the air and then flipped it down and told Kao he was busy and had something that needed his immediate attention. He went to the back of the store where he picked up the phone and dialed the police.

The police was understaffed and said they would send one of their detectives. It was Captain Jaks who asked for Bert or Jay to stop by the store. He was still angry about losing Bert. Jay, not so much; it was just a matter of time before he transferred to either another division or jurisdiction.

The phone call was a little odd, but factual. Jay and Bert were not as busy as everyone else. Jay had just picked up Charlie from the jail as he was finally released. He would be with Charlie, under witness detail, until the FBI got involved and had an agent on full-time witness protection. He looked at Charlie who was riding next to him. He nodded his head. "We will take the call," said Jay. Their car was no longer a squad car but a regular sedan. Jay had put the lights on top of the car before leaving the station. This was the first time he had to use them.

They arrived at Brooker's to find Pascal waiting on the curb with his elbows on his knees. He had finished making his phone calls except to his mom. He had no idea what he was going to tell her. Maybe she would be impressed with his conscience, but it was such a dumb thing to do to begin with that he doubted it.

Mr. Kower came out to meet Jay. Pascal was already standing. Mr. Kower showed him the shoes and the note. Jay stared at Pascal in disbelief. "Seriously, after two years," said Jay. "You were protesting, rioting, and looting?" he asked Jay.

Pascal knew better than to say anything or to correct Jay and let him know that he was only protesting and looting and it was only Brooker's for which he was there. Charlie was listening with the window down. *Smart boy,*

Charlie thought, *not defending himself.* Jay shook his head. "So what do you want to do, Mr. Kower?" Jay asked. "Do you want to press charges?" He didn't wait for an answer before trying to win over Mr. Kower. "He returned the item. Was this the only item?" asked Jay turning back to Pascal. Pascal said it was.

There were only a few yards between them and Pascal. Mr. Kower walked up to Pascal and grinned. "Yes, I want to press charges. Definitely, I want to press charges," said Mr. Kower.

The window was open and Charlie's arm was hanging out of it with his fingers tapping on the side of the car. Charlie said, "Oh man," and dropped his head. Jay made a face. Charlie withdrew his hand back inside the car. "Sir, you are definitely within your rights to do so. There is no statute of limitations on this. Though many of the looters and rioters were arrested and released without being charged. They did not return their items like Pascal, which makes this still prosecutable." Mr. Kower looked down shaking his head. There was either another "Oh man" from the car, or an "Amen." Jay was not sure what he had heard from what should have been a silent witness. Charlie wanted to say, *Dumb, dumb, dumb,* for returning the shoes in the first place but instead there it was, his words came out clearer and bolder.

There was a look like that of a deer in the headlights from Jay. The arm and part of Charlie's body returned from inside the car. He instead he shouted, "Luke 15:7—In the same way, I tell you that there will be more joy in heaven over one sinner who repents than over ninety-nine righteous ones who do not need to repent." Jay looked at him with his eyebrows bent. Charlie shrugged, and there it was again. "Luke 15:10—Likewise, I say unto you, there is joy in the presence of the angels of God over one sinner that repenteth," said Charlie.

Jay was red-faced when he asked Charlie if he was done. Charlie again shrugged his shoulders, rolled up his window, and put his head in his hands.

Mr. Kower, although he was not a Christian, was put off guard. Jay had one more piece of information that might help Pascal's case. "So how many more of these little bags do you have to deliver today?" asked Jay. Pascal said that was the only one. Jay then asked if he could search his car. It was always, always a bag of worms, but he asked anyway. Pascal, like everyone else, said he had nothing to hide.

The car was neatly kept. He looked in the trunk, the back seat, the front seat, and the dash. There were no signs of drugs or other items to be returned. To Jay that was a small miracle, and he realized he really liked this kid. He shook his head at Mr. Kower, letting him know his car was clean.

Mr. Kower walked back and forth and then up to Pascal, who had been silently praying. "You are really sorry? That was a hard time for all of us." asked Mr. Kower.

Pascal stood eye to eye with Mr. Kower. "I am," said Pascal. "I am really, really sorry for everything that happened to your store." Mr. Kower turned and shook his head at Jay. Jay was not sure exactly what that meant but had a good guess. Jay approached Pascal, now looking at him square in the eyes.

Mr. Kower came up behind Jay. He whispered, "It's okay, today is the kid's lucky day." and then walked inside his shop.

The car that was behind Jay's sedan was double-parked. Jay was not going to split hairs since he already figured it was Pascal's. He was in hurry to get in and out. Jay wanted to tell him that he did right, but instead he handed him his card and told him if he needed anything to call him. Pascal lifted up the card with a huge smile and said thanks. He rapped on Charlie's window and waved. He got into his car with a clear conscience and drove back home to whatever dinner his mom had cooked him that night.

Chapter Seven

The Tropical Oasis

There were not too many places to hide for Belmont. His real name was Hudson Rivers. He stared at his picture of Pauline. She was neither cute nor beautiful. How was it that she was Charlie's undoing? Charlie could have been his partner until Hudson tired of him. It was the least of his problems now.

He looked at his watch. Right on time, Captain Jaks sat across from him. He had already surveyed his surroundings, and nothing stuck out to him as abnormal.

The waitress came by and asked them if they wanted anything to drink. Captain Jaks said the Tropical mai tai, and Hudson said water. "When in Rome?" said Captain Jaks. "So how did you lose them and where are going to go now?" he asked.

Hudson was nervous. He had never been so close to being caught in his career. He had enough stashed away to quit and live quietly and comfortably for the rest of his life, but he was not sure if he would ever be safe. He needed more information.

The mai tai was perfect. Captain Jaks looked at the man across the table and wondered how he could get so clumsy. Bert and Jay had connected all but one of the dots, and he was it. "Jaks, I am going to finish the job," said Hudson. "Let them know this is not over."

The waitress came back for their order. Jaks ordered a poke bowl, and Hudson ordered fish tacos. Jaks tilted his head with his mouth a little open. He did not speak quickly. He played with his silverware on the table. He knew he was no match for Hudson and would not pretend to be, yet he was not afraid to be bold.

The napkin fell to the ground. Jaks knew better than to make any sudden moves so he left it there. "You've burned out," said Jaks. "Don't come back to the United States unless you want to get caught. Damn it, you are on all sorts of cameras, and people actually know you."

Cameras were always the problem. Hudson used them for espionage, and they were the first thing he looked for when he entered in any building. It came to him quickly: Christmas lights. Charlie had not just put up lights but also cameras. It was how he knew Hudson was at Pauline's that night, a knight in shining armor! No matter; he should be going away for life. "I can handle it," said Hudson. "Charlie is in prison and no one else should be able to connect me. He won't be safe there. So no one still knows to be looking for me. No one knows who I was working for or that there was a hit on one of the officers. I have cleaned up my loose ends."

They talked about trivial things while locals were being seated. The food finally came. The tacos were perfect. The poke bowl did not have the deep red tuna that Captain Jaks preferred, but what did he expect? It was in the South Pacific. He was taking the wife and kids to Hawaii over the weekend, which would meet all his expectations. "All right," he said, "you need to go somewhere and disappear. Charlie did not hang. Those loose ends will testify. No, they may not know who contacted you, but they know for whom. You had Charlie spy on both Pauline and Bert. They know what you do and that you're ex-military now. They do know who you are. Not to mention, your company lost faith in you, not just one hit but two."

This time it was Hudson's turn to turn around and give the invisible man the finger. He just heard his own funeral march, except guys like him don't get that luxury. No wonder he could not find his target; they found the "newspaper man." The island was a death sentence. Every hour he was there was 10 percent more chance that he would not be able to leave. Jaks had come to warn him, but why?

The Tropical Oasis was not five-star, but there were no five-star resorts on the island. Derby would not stay anyway. He was anxious to leave the island and get back to family.

Time to call it quits. This was it. He would make this hit, which was more important to the company in exchange for dropping the hit on Bert. Things were getting complex.

Derby did not like working with partners, especially Hudson. It was a variable in the equation that he could count on complicating things in the end. Hudson did not know how to communicate. He had rules in the beginning that he did not follow in the end. He often talked about one of his golden rules or some other type of rule, only to break them. His tactical way of cleaning things up got muddled with revenge. Derby wondered if Hudson knew that his end was imminent. Hell, if all of their ends weren't closing in on them like a noose tightening around their collective necks. He was being too pensive, but it continued. When did he start working for the bad guy, solely? When did he become the bad guy?

Derby was looking to hang it up. He hated the organization for which it stood, the manipulation of government agencies as well as legislative bodies. He was a patriot. The government still recruited him for employment from time to time, but if things did not go smoothly he would be on the nation's most wanted list. He switched his scope from Captain Jaks. He took aim at Hudson's heart and was waiting for the sign, which never came.

★★★

It was official. Pauline would need a plus-one. She had her invite stuck between the magnet and the refrigerator. Seth was out of the picture. Apparently, Bert no longer was trying to befriend him, and he stopped showing up at church. She knew that night when Charlie showed up that she had nothing in common with him. It would have to be Bert, although it would have to be as friends. He was no longer interested in her, even though he stopped by more often than not. She would stop by his house, but if he had any spare time, he was at hers. His new job kept him busy. He even traveled to Texas, Fort Worth, how exciting she thought. She wanted to come by and see his new office but knew it would not be a good idea.

The police station was off limits when they were dating. Bert would tell her it was too much commotion, and he was mostly not there, so she had stopped dropping things off. Then, when he asked if she wanted to get together with Jay and his wife and kids, she was beside herself with excitement. She tried to stay composed and limited herself to four questions about the Truitts. A normal person would only have asked two but she was not normal. She was extra, but knowing she was extra was half the battle.

That night Bert had planned to stop by for, as he put it, "an evening of fun." He was even bringing dinner. Pauline would pop the question. She hoped Bert would say yes to being her plus-one. He would have to wear something suitable, but that would not be a problem as she pictured him in what he'd worn to the police Christmas function last year.

There was the knock. She went to the door and there was Lucy and Charlie and her father. Charlie had picked up Lucy at the airport. Her father flew with her to meet Charlie. Although Charlie wanted to come by and visit, his motives were hidden.

The cameras were mostly on the outside of the house, but there were two on the inside that Charlie had to steal back. Whether he decided to tell Pauline was another matter. As most information on everything pertaining to the case was classified, he really could not tell her much other than he had installed cameras in her house, which would make him a stalker. He would not be able to explain himself and so would have to leave it there. He decided to take his chances at getting caught taking back the cameras.

Lucy knew only a few details and was not allowed to elaborate on them. Her father, who carried a higher clearance although it was not required as a police officer, knew more than anyone else. Texas was also considering a similar program to that of their state for interstate law enforcement, but he had retained his clearances from a previous vocation when did not live in Texas and worked closer to the police station downtown in a government building.

She invited them inside her home. The large Texan cop took off his hat and bowed his head and smiled. "Howdy, I'm Lucy's dad." She was not the swooning type, but she was almost fell to her knees. It might have been not obvious to most, but it was to Lucy. She looked down and took a step closer to Charlie. Pauline's only thought was *Plus-one, please?*

The hugs came first. Pauline hugged Lucy, which was a little uncomfortable for Lucy, especially in front of her dad, but after the first couple seconds she melted into Pauline's arms. Charlie hugged the hardest, and Pauline hugged hard back. Lucy's dad opened his arms widely, but Pauline shook her head. Her face turned all shades of crimson. She only offered a fist bump. Lucy chuckled.

Their shoes and boots were left by the front door, part of a West Coast custom which was unfamiliar to Pauline. They adjourned to the downstairs family room next to the kitchen. "I have missed you all so much. Not you," she said to Lucy's dad with a wink. "What can I get you to drink, and have you eaten anything today?" she asked. "By the way, I am Pauline. Do you go by something else other than Lucy's dad?" She tried to laugh casually. It came out more like that of a gurgling sound, to which everyone did a double-take. Pauline heard it too but chose to ignore it.

The white leather recliner fit his build well. He had already pulled back on the recliner so his feet were propped up. "My name is Rex, short for Rex, but I go by Rex or Big Tex." said Rex and grinned and laughed a hardy laugh. Lucy smiled. She loved her dad. Pauline forced a giggle, but this time it was more distinguishable as such.

Charlie gulped. He hated any situation where anyone embarrassed themselves. It was even more extreme when it involved older people and everyone in this room was over thirty, except for him and Lucy. He and Lucy exchanged looks. Lucy was not sure why, since for her, it was normal for her father to be funny.

Charlie was happy to excuse himself and be of assistance. "I'll help," he offered. He pointed to Lucy's dad first, who said he would have a vodka tonic; again with the humor. "Sweetened ice tea it is," said Charlie and then asked if Pauline had sweetened ice tea, which she did not. They settled on an Arnie Palmer, half tea and half lemonade, which became the choice for everyone.

Charlie looked in the refrigerator and pulled out cans of Arnie Palmer. "What does everyone want to eat?" said Pauline. It was obvious she was struggling. Charlie suggested sandwiches. He opened the fridge again and looked in the meat drawer to find only cheese slices.

That put it down to grilled cheeses. He looked around for bread, but there was none. He opened the freezer to find frozen lasagna.

The lasagna took seventy minutes to cook, which would be too long, but the choices were slim to none. "This looks good," said Charlie. Pauline was secretly elated that he found anything at all that would be fit for company.

It was the only lasagna left in the freezer. She intentionally had not gone to the store, since Bert was bringing dinner. Pauline nodded. Charlie prepped the oven and then pulled the ingredients for a salad out of the refrigerator. "Lasagna it is." he said. He quickly made a hand-tossed salad and stuck it back into the fridge. He looked for a frozen loaf of bread or biscuits to add, but there were none. The meal was fine without it, he reasoned. He was tempted to make biscuits from scratch but was not sure if Pauline even had flour at this point. Pauline came into the kitchen to see if she could be of assistance. "Hey, I got this. You go sit down." he said.

Two cans were handed to Pauline, and Charlie followed with Lucy's Arnie Palmers. He went back into the kitchen and quickly removed the camera from on top of the refrigerator. The bottom half was covered with dust. He put it in his pocket. He slid the pan of lasagna in the preheated oven and grabbed his drink off the counter top. *One down and one to go*, he thought to himself.

As everyone made their way to the table to eat, Rex asked where the bathroom was and pointed down the hallway to Charlie. Pauline was in the kitchen pulling out the lasagna. "It's around the corner," said Charlie. "You passed it on the way." He came to see at what Rex was pointing at, but Rex just wanted Charlie's ear.

Lucy's eyes were on her dad. He was acting suspiciously, but he made a face at Lucy so she turned around. "Where is one of the cameras? I can help," said Rex. He pointed to the bookshelf in the downstairs family room next to the walk-in pantry. "I'll get them outside after dinner and you grab it, plan?" said Rex. Charlie was thankful for Rex's help. He forgot that Rex had been filled in more than anyone else.

The lasagna was getting tiresome for Pauline, but she enjoyed her piece, just not as much as if it was not a staple. Lucy, Pauline, and Rex went outside to see the backyard at the prompting of Rex. Charlie snatched the last camera from the bookshelf.

The lights turned on again for Pauline, but it was not quite nightfall yet, so it was not as impressive. When they returned from touring the backyard, Charlie was doing the dishes. "Great job on the landscaping," Rex said to Lucy and Charlie. They both said it was no big deal at the same time and laughed. "It was a pleasure meeting you, Pauline," said Rex. "Lucy has had only kind words to say about you. I will be here for at least another two weeks. I have some business to which I will be attending. I hope to see you again at some time before I leave for Fort Worth."

They left, and Pauline was thankful that they were fine. She had not seen Charlie after he had finished the front yard, which was unlike him. She had spent some time praying and even fasting for them. She felt honored that Lucy brought her father to meet her with Charlie, and they came straightway from the airport.

It was shortly thereafter that Bert arrived and greeted Pauline with a kiss on her cheek. He had Italian food in his arms along with some flowers. She took them from him and thanked him. There were fall flowers with sunflowers in the middle. She put them in a vase with water on the kitchen counter between the sunroom and the actual kitchen. "They are beautiful. I can't remember the last time someone brought me flowers. "Oh, that's right." She paused. Bert already knew what she was going to say. "It was my birthday, and you brought me a beautiful bouquet of mixed flowers with baby's breath and roses."

Bert looked down. "You have a good memory." He had been thinking of asking someone out from his church, but he wanted to be honest and up-front with Pauline before he did. He knew that timing was everything, and she was honest with him. If she had no intentions of dating him again, then he needed to go in a different direction.

Pauline was on another wavelength. She knew what she wanted to ask him but did not know how to ask it.

Alexa was always good for music. She asked Alexa to play an artist she knew they both liked. "I have something I want to ask you," she said. Bert was afraid it would be something related to what had been going on with work. He was worried about the overflow and how it had already affected Pauline. He owed her an explanation for something but would wait until the end of the evening. She of course was only concerned about her plus-one. "Would you be my plus-one to my cousin's wedding?" said Pauline.

The candles were kept in the top drawer. He retrieved an apple cinnamon and put it on top of the counter. He already started to take the manicotti and ravioli out of their containers. "Yes, so is it a wine night or not?" said Bert. He had smelled Italian food as soon as he entered the kitchen. "Did you already have Italian? I think I smell lasagna." He plated the Italian food with the bread and salad.

The corkscrew was in the drawer next to the candles. She held up two bottles from which to choose. He chose the same Cabernet that they had previously and pulled out the corkscrew.

They had it down to a science in the kitchen when they were together. "Yes, we have to celebrate. I have my plus-one." said Pauline. Bert laughed. "And yes, I fixed lasagna for Charlie, Lucy, and her father for lunch. They left not long ago."

The wine was poured into two large wine glasses but only a quarter full. "You have not seen Seth in a while, have you?" she said. "Are you worried about him? I am not going to have him over here anymore. There is something about him." She helped herself to one of the glasses of wine. She took a rather large swallow. Bert stared at her and wished he had been there that night.

He took the other glass off the counter and held it in his hand. "I found out some things about him. I ran a check, and he has a criminal background. You need to call me if you see him again." He wanted to tell her that they were tracking him, but it would have set off far too many alarms. She was intrigued.

The Italian food smelled good even though she had just eaten a few hours ago. She went and stood beside him and leaned against the counter. "So what else can you tell me, anything?" said Pauline.

She catches on quick, Bert thought. He said, "Not much." Most people might have got their feelings hurt over something like that, but she was more practical than most.

"I figure I am probably safer that way," she said. "The less I know, the less I will react if something does come to light, but when you can, do tell me. I can do a lot with the information I am told." He chuckled.

The wine was smooth like the last bottle they had. Bert took a sip. "Like what? Write about it?" He looked down at Pauline and kissed her. It was a good lead-in to what he wanted to ask, but he did not need to ask it. She set her wine down and kissed him the way they used to kiss. He had questions, but they could wait for a minute.

The water glasses were the only thing not set out. She turned around. He whispered in her ear. She turned back around and said, "Yes. We can start this over again. I don't want to be with anyone else besides you, and that includes just me. I won't do what I did again and I will be a better friend."

He kissed her again and whispered once more in her ear, "Thank you."

The sunroom was lit up with white light strung from the top of the room. They decided to eat in the sunroom. He had one more thing to get off his chest. "You are my best friend," Bert said. "I think you know that, and you should know that." He took her hand. "You are a good friend. However, if you think you can be a better friend, well, I am looking forward to it."

Pauline laughed and smacked his hand. Then she put her head on his shoulder.

★★★

The next morning everything changed except for Pauline's and Bert's relationship. "So you're in a good mood today," said Jay. Bert nodded in agreement. He

167

could not wait to confide in Jay. Jay handed him his coffee. "I hope it stays that way," said Jay. He pointed to the woman sauntering across the office. Sara waved. Jay made a coughing sound, and at the same time he said, "On our team." It was to keep Bert from being blindsided.

The dispatcher had been promoted. They had to wait for her to get her clearances before she was able to transfer floors. Sara shook Bert's hand like a professional. "Oh coffee", she said. "Is this for everyone? I suppose it's for everyone in the conference room." she said as she helped herself. "So we are supposed to meet in fifteen minutes?" she asked. "DC is on his way."

There it was, she was there for Detective Captain Murphy. She was going to ask an amazing amount of annoying questions; she was extra. In fact it seemed everything she said was a question, most of them rhetorical. "So welcome aboard." said Bert. "It's the three of us plus DC, and yes that is our nickname for Detective Captain Murphy. Try not to ask so many questions, or if you do, ask Jay. He knows more than the rest of us." He laughed, but Sara found it insulting.

The coffee machine was popular. Some of the agencies had moved into their departmental sections of the office. Jay was waiting in line for his second cup of coffee. He turned around and gave Sara a thumbs-up and pointed to himself. "I am the only one who is up on some of the technology." he said.

DC, Detective Captain Murphy, stepped off the elevator and headed toward the conference room. Sara looked at Bert. "So that's what you meant by trying not to ask so many questions—because you don't have the answers?", asked Sara. Bert did not answer and would not answer. It was better that way, he thought. Eventually she would get it. She had to get it.

The coffee line in the conference room was down to five. People from the other side of the office came to get their cup of joe from the expresso machine. DC did the math. If everyone spent two minutes getting their coffee and leaving it would be fifteen minutes into their meeting time.

The annoyance factor rose. "Hey," said DC, "there is a Keurig over on the other side of the office. Go!" Then he turned to Sara and held out his hand. "Welcome, Sara.", he said.

The line shortened quickly to only two; Sara was the enforcer. She comically shoed the last person away and helped herself to another cup of coffee before sitting down. She wished she had a pastry to go with her coffee. Next time she thought. DC eventually helped himself to a cup of espresso with Bert behind him.

In time, everyone found their places. DC placed folders in front of them. The folders had been pulled out of the secured document center.

It was all falling together. Bert immediately started to underline information as he paged through some of the documents. He was use to memorizing details for some of his cases but now he had his clearances he was able to hold on to the paper a little longer.

The information was easy to disseminate. "We have some updates on our main case file. Sara, try not to ask too many questions, or save them for later. Jay will be your main point of contact.", said DC. *I'm not dumb. That is not why I was hired.* Jay raised his cup of coffee toward Sara, who was across the table from him. *Still, this is neat,* thought Sara, but she was pretty sure she was being disrespected.

Everyone was now on the same page. DC slid them additional folders across the table. Sara did not get one, but she understood; her position was not similar to that of detective. She was an information analyst who was to help with logistics. She was taking copious notes. "It's okay, boss. You'll catch me next time," she said. The DC said nothing except that the information was for not a current case and pertained only to Bert and Jay.

The information was lumped together with pictures, dates, and times, phone records and intel sourced from different federal databases. The first picture was of Captain Jaks with Hudson Rivers sitting in a restaurant together. Sara gasped, and the others swore. It was as if stakes were driven right into Jay's and Bert's hearts. Captain Jaks was one of the good guys. He was one of *them.* There were times when Bert had questioned his positions in dealing with other departments and the occasional case, but the betrayal of all, none could explain. They all needed a minute. Jay and Bert looked hard at the picture, hoping it would magically transform into someone who looked like him, an imposter, but unfortunately there were several other photos to follow.

It was a minute. Jay grabbed a trash can and tried not to throw up which initiated a gag response from Sara. Bert sobbed as if he was at a wake. They needed to know why. It couldn't remain a mystery.

Feelings aside, it was hard to understand. Their emotions were caught up in the case. They definitely were not impartial. They still needed to proceed with no option to recluse themselves since they were only four working the case and they all knew Jaks. Sara was now crying. Bert carried a handkerchief that he was not using and it to Sara.

The reaction was a surprise. The DC was not sure how this would play out, but he hadn't thought it would be a funeral. "Okay, we need to carry on and put on our professional face and hat." Sara blew her nose. The information was multifaceted and had many directions they could follow, but time was not on their side. They needed to home in on what not only needed to be done but where to go next with the information that would be obtained. "We have this," said Jay. He threw up one last time and took a drink of water. He wiped his mouth on his sleeve and gave the detective captain a thumbs-up. He nodded.

The typed page of details had highlights of events and meetings that Captain Jaks attended and who was there. Others might be implicated, but there was no proof yet. "I hate to ask this, but if you are too emotionally bonded to this case, I need to relinquish your duties to other detectives from the agency," said the DC. Sara shook her head and stood up to leave. "Not you, Sara, but it would be good if you could pull it together. Is that how you ran the dispatch?"

She grimaced and sat back down. She said, "Sorry, boss," and wrote something in her notebook.

Jay and Bert looked at each other. There was no doubt that they were affected by the information, but they did not want to walk away. Bert said, "It will take time for me and I am guessing Jay to not only digest what you are telling us but also to mourn properly. As far as objectivity, I can only speak for myself, but I can go forward with this case." Jay said that he would also be able to be objective.

They both had more questions. Bert asked why they weren't able to pick up Hudson when they followed him to the island. It was playing out like a Hollywood movie.

The pacing across the floor started with the flood of emotions. Captain Murphy paced the floor and explained what he knew. "He hired a double. They thought that he was still on the island, but they searched the island, and there was no trace. The agency tracked the local small ships, cruise ships, and airlines, but to no avail. They think it was possible that he may have taken a small boat out and transferred to another boat or got off at another small island. They have checked most of the surrounding islands and still have not been able to find Hudson."

★★★

Derby could not sleep that night. Why did he not get the sign to make the hit? If he walked away, he might be able to make it. He knew if he got too close it would be him alone that would be on the run. Otherwise he and his wife had a plan. Although she did not know what exactly it was that he did, she trusted him. It would be the family that would go and eventually meet up with him. Right now, he was still off the grid as far as the knowledge from his informants. His source knew where he was but not for long. He was good at disappearing after a job.

As he lay in bed thinking about his next play, he got a text. *They're on the way to airport. Take them both out.* He was not sure what had changed; it was supposed to be in order, a one and then a two, with time in between, but he did not care. He decided he was out. He took out his burner and sent a text to his wife. *I'll see you soon.*

The message to his wife would have no reply. She did as she had been directed. She woke the kids. "Daddy needs us," she said, and that was all they needed to hear.

They pulled out their suitcases from under their beds and packed. They whispered to each other, although the protocol was not to use words.

A car pulled up in front of the house. She looked through her blinds. The headlights switched on and off. They pulled their suitcases out to the curb.

There he was. A man that she knew from her husband's group of friends picked up the luggage and put it in the trunk as their family piled into the car. "Everything will be okay," said one of Derby's informants.

Chapter Eight

One Life

The happiness was draining quickly. It had been a week, but Bert was still processing the betrayal. He was sluggish and hard to be around, but in this situation, Pauline was at her best. "Drink this," she said and gave him some chamomile tea. She had finally made it to the grocery store a couple of days earlier and procured the ingredients to make a ham and cheese sandwich with her own version of a mustard dressing. "I know you can't talk about it, but I bet it was hell," she said. They prayed together, and she let him just be while she typed.

> Kara was no longer in her own little world. She left the safety of their condo and her friends to find her sister. She thought she would come back, but it was going on a year. Her chances of finding Naomi were getting less and less as time passed, but still she did not feel like the Lord was telling her that Naomi was no more, just that there was a lot to be explained.

She wandered the streets during the day, and it was like this as in the beginning she lost her way. Once again she wished Naomi was with her so they would be lost together. She was too tired to cry. She sat down by a tree and took out a piece of bread and ate like a starving person.

Bert knew he could mope by himself at his own place; hers was not nicer, but having her company was much better than being alone and watching television. Pauline's house was barely decorated. The walls had not been painted since she first moved in. There were no throw pillows on the white leather furniture or books in the wooden bookcases by the fireplace.

It was not tranquil or quaint. Pauline's interior design limitations were obvious. There were just a few odds and ends that did not quite make sense. The sunroom was the only room in the house that looked like something out of a magazine with large blue ceramic floor tiles. It had expensive patio furniture with pillows and plants galore.

The good Lord provided the sunlight through the large glass windows to brighten the place up. "I want to get married," Bert said. "I know we disagree on logistics, but we love each other. I want to move on with our life together. This is good, but I need to be with you. Nothing would make me happier."

The surprise was obvious. Pauline was happy with what they had and wouldn't trade it, but the next step was scary. She tried to rationalize it, but her heartbeat would not calm down so she could think.

Bert went on, "We will get through the nervousness together. You don't have to say yes now—this isn't a proposal. I just wanted to talk about it."

It might have been cheating—that is, talking about it first before asking her to marry him—but he had prayed about it and felt this was the right approach. She needed him to help her process even if she did not know it or admit to it. He grabbed her hand and could feel her anxiety.

They sat on the couch and talked about marriage. Pauline was warming to the idea. It was never something they had talked about before, but it was what Bert fervently desired. He wanted to start their lives together soon, tomorrow if possible. Pauline was not sure if it was because he felt some sort of impending doom or he was a bit depressed. She was too insecure to see Bert was desperate to be with her and fantasized about growing older together.

She, on the other hand, was more practical about the matter. She knew they were both getting older and had hoped to have been married by now. She put her hand on his arm and stared at him while he held his chamomile tea and spoke. At times, his gaze would be fixed straight ahead but his head slightly down. He was a "steady Eddie," a character she would write about in one of her books. He was sturdy as the day is long. He never made anything complicated. She would have told him that she had her reservations, but what would that have helped? "I get it," said Pauline. He needed this, and she felt it too.

Bert was a thinker, always meditating on something, but either she knew what he was thinking or she was able to break through the ice before he withdrew within himself and from others. What she liked about him the most was their fellowship, and he was fun. They both did not drink much, so their fun did not come from carousing. Most of their activities came from venturing out together; it was a younger person's "beer and skittles." They loved to be outside. Bert liked to fish, hike, kayak, swim, hunt, and almost everything else. He kept fit but was not a health nut. Even errands were enjoyable.

The more Pauline thought about him, the more she liked him. She had never been fishing, but he said he wanted to take her. As far as 'cons', they did not agree on their church or where to live. Although they both had in common their love for their city and state, neither wanted to give up their home. She presumed as far as cons versus pros, it could be worse. If she wished to be selfish or manipulative, she could make her wishes his concessions, but it seemed foul to start a marriage that way.

"So we are agreed," he said, leaned over, and kissed her on her cheek. Then he stood up. She could see the wheels still turning inside his head. She walked him to the door. "We are going to not only be better together but will have as our raison d'être to be one in Him." *Powerful*, she thought. She reminded him not forget about the Truitts the following night.

★★★

Hawaii was great. It had to be. Captain Jaks and the kids and his wife vacationed in style, whether they could afford it or not. He took the elevator up to the top floor but did not have access to get off on that floor. A cleared construction worker was going down as he was coming up. The worker stepped into the elevator as Jaks stepped out, not bothering to look for a keycard or another type of identification that would give access to the top floor.

There he was face to face with the DC. He had his arms in front of him with his wrists together—*as if he could have the luxury of not being cuffed behind his back*, the DC thought. No-one had seen Detective Captain Murphy lose his cool, until that moment. He gritted his teeth, stuck out his chest, and made a growling noise that came from deep inside of him. He wanted to throw a punch and pulled his right hand back as if it was on the way, but he stopped and said, "You have the right," as he handcuffed his wrists and continued.

Captain Jaks had a plan; it was called turning state's witness. He needed protection for his family. Had he walked onto his floor, he would have been greeted with the normal enthusiasm, for no one knew. He would have had time, the district attorney's office would have to prove wrongdoing, and that would take work unless they came across someone in the company who was willing to talk with no incentive which was equivalent to a snowball's chance in Hades. There was a bigger threat than the DA breathing down his neck. The previous night he had dreamed he had a laser pointed at his head and one at his heart, and then more appeared. He woke in a deep sweat. His wife knew something was wrong, but he said it was just the job.

He realized the dream was accurate. With everything unraveling he could be the one man to bring down the company. It all made sense. The company did not tell him to bring Belmont in, but only to meet with him. That's why he warned Belmont; they were the same, wanted. He knew the company. He was moving up in the company. He knew every little detail on a local level that was covered up because he was part of it, and he also knew about Bert. In truth he was hoping he could protect Bert, but no one would believe him. He could do right. No one had to convince him it was the right thing to do to turn on the company. He was tough enough to do the time, whatever the cost, but if he was dead, there would be no clean slate. He only had one life.

In a matter of minutes two federal agents showed up. "We'll take him from here," said Agent Becks. The DC assumed Captain Jaks would be safe, but he had uneasy feeling. Apparently Jaks knew he was not safe, or he would not have shown up on the top floor. Jaks knew that the DC had to be the one to arrest him.

It was happening. The DC sent a text to another agent he worked closely with and asked him to watch for Jaks. He walked Jaks to the elevator and told Jaks he would be in contact and added a nasty name. The DC watched as the elevator closed.

★★★

The Truitts' house was in the sticks. It was not hard to find if you had directions. It was a modest house on a decent piece of land. It overlooked a river and was mostly wooded. Pauline was beside herself when Bert arrived at her house. She greeted him with a kiss this time. It was odd having things beings so familiar and yet new. "Do you love me?" she asked. She was not sure where the question came from, but all of sudden it was important. He confirmed with the simple words *I love you*, spoken without emotion. There were no doubt or hesitation. It was as if, it had always been true.

The ride out to the Truitts' house was at least forty minutes, but it went by quickly for Pauline, who talked incessantly about current events for the entire car ride. She had been reading up in case it came up in conversation with the Truitts. The car ride did not seem as short for Bert, who would turn on the radio just to have it turned down by Pauline so she could continue discussing politics or anything else that rolled into her head. By the time they reached the house, Bert was ready to jump out of the car, but instead he turned it off, took the keys out of the ignition, and leaned over and kissed Pauline on the lips. "Are you ready to meet the Truitts?" he asked. She was nervous, but nervousness aside, she was excited.

The home had a rustic vibe. The architecture was that of American Craftsman matched by its setting in the deep woods by the river. It had a low-pitched roof, overhanging eaves, and a large front porch that spanned the front of the house. Most of the outside of the house was painted a light taupe. It gave Pauline a very warm feeling.

The door opened wide, and two young children escaped the house. They waited for Bert to step out of the car to give him a hug. When Pauline then stepped out of the car, the two escapees ran around the car and hugged her as well. "So who do I thank for this honor?" asked Pauline. They looked at each other and shrugged. Then the older girl pointed to the younger girl, who had no expression on her face, and they went back to their parents who were now waiting on the front stoop. "Breanna and Heather," called Jeanna, placing her hands on one head and then the other.

They entered the house with thanksgiving. Pauline felt the love as soon as she stepped across the threshold. Breanna and Heather wanted to show Bert several things that they had been working on for school. "I homeschool, but not alone. It is a type of co-op that we do with the church, which is actually part of a larger international program," said Jeanna. "The girls are proud of the schoolwork they have done, so they like to show it off. They will debate you on everything if they are allowed. That is another critical part of their education, being able to discuss openly and defend their positions on their beliefs as well as their opinions. It is a healthy program."

Children were not something that Pauline had cared to discuss in the past. It was a parting of ways between herself and those of her friends who had gotten engaged and married and then gone on to have children. "That's good.", said Pauline. She felt as if those friends were descending downhill, and she could not catch them. They were in different stages of their lives in different directions.

The inside of the house matched the American Craftsman style. It had cherry-stained exposed rafters that could be seen when entering the house. It was an open floor plan. You could see through to the back of the house and out onto the deck with mostly windows on the backside of the house. It even had a touch of Frank Floyd Wright architecture as well, with the light coming in from the back and straight lines. The deck was also contemporary, as it was concrete and not wood with stairs going down into the yard.

Time to talk. Pauline thought about how hard it must be for Jeanna to live out in the country by herself while homeschooling the kids all day. Also being a detective's wife could be lonely.

Marriage and children, Pauline felt the strain in their own relationship without being wed and having children. They sat down on their oversized La-Z-Boy sofa with drinks in hand. Pauline was relieved when Jeanna told her and Jay were looking at homes closer to the station. She almost spilt her drink with excitement. She started to move closer on the sofa to Jeanna to tell her that she thought it was a great idea for social reasons, but she caught herself.

Originally, that was not the plan for them. Jenna explained the family was going to move further away to a different precinct until Jay was promoted. "So our plans were to still move farther away to something that was more affordable," Jeanna said, "but with the promotion came a pay grade differential in salary. The fact that Jay already had clearances meant he could negotiate a little more so we can afford something closer to work in a different county." Jeanna went to get another beer.

The window was open in the kitchen, and the ashtray was full. "I'm just having a smoke," said Jeanna. "Do you smoke? It's a filthy habit. I know I should quit." She took a puff. Pauline only knew she had found a new friend. "I try not to smoke around the kids."

The conversation went on until Breanna and Heather came down and wondered how much longer until dinner. Jay and Bert joined everyone in the kitchen. "Guess I had better throw something on the grill," said Jay. Jeanna set out some hummus and vegetables, and the girls helped themselves. Jay went and opened the fridge. "So, honey, what else did you want me to throw on with the steaks?" asked Jay.

The kitchen also had a rustic feel. The cabinets were restored cherrywood. There was a prominent beam that ran the length of the ceiling which was higher than the other ceilings in the house. The farmhouse sink was center to the kitchen.

It was behind the large island and was in front of two adjoining windows that had longer panes and overlooked the backyard. It was such a beautiful house that Pauline thought it nearly contended with her home.

Jeanna went to the fridge and pulled out four dishes covered in foil. "These are the potatoes. These are the vegetables for one of the sides. These are the onions and peppers for the steaks," she said as she set them all on a pan. "Last, these are the mushrooms." She picked up the pan and waited.

Jay smiled at Jeanna. He adored his wife, but she had been pulling away from him. It started before his promotion.

The deck was more of a large patio on stilts. Decks, especially on a house like his, should be normal and not contemporary concrete. Bert had told Jay so on many occasion. As Jay opened the grill, which had already been prepped, Bert told a couple of jokes, but Jay barely laughed. He told him about Pauline and their decision to get married, but it was obvious that Jay had something else on his mind.

"Hey, Bert," said Jay. It always started with "hey" if was going to be serious and require special attention. It was similar to the situation between Ernie and Bert on Sesame Street. After "Hey, Bert," you never knew what was coming next with Ernie; it was usually something that would not agree with him.

Bert set his lemonade down on the side shelf of the grill. "What is it?" he asked. Jay said it wasn't anything and they could talk about it later. "It's a nice night," Bert said and sipped his drink before setting it back down. They could see the river from the deck, and the lights from different houses twinkled in the distance. "I bet the view is something at Christmastime with all the lights," said Bert. Jay said yeah and took a gulp of his beer. It would have been impressive with the quiet sounds of nature if they did not hear Pauline and Jeanna talking in the background.

The sound of water in the distance was relaxing, but Jay was anything but. "Bert, I never meant to hurt anyone, but I have been involved in some things that I am not proud of, especially now. It was for the bigger good." Bert made a joke and asked if he would need to escort him away in handcuffs after he finished his confession. He was warning Jay to be careful of what he was going to say next. "I worked with Jaks on a couple of our arrests. I went back to some of these organizations and negotiated information. I did not want to keep this from you any longer. You've been a good partner," said Jay.

The fight was on, Bert looked away and then came back with a right hook which, had it landed, would have been fine for Jay. He loved a good fight and never lost one yet, but he knew Bert well enough that he could predict what came next in most situations. It was what he did, so he dodged the blow. The second shot landed. Jay licked his lip and felt his jaw jar. That hurt. It brought him back to eighth grade, maybe his teenager years. He smiled.

This would be entertaining to see what his old friend Bert had to give if the matter at hand was not so serious. In the past, he and his brothers fought all the time. His dad said it was healthy. His mom had him in therapy for most of his life. True to form, it was how they established dominance and communicated, but that was then, and this was now.

At some point he could get ticked off, and then it would be over; Bert would beg for mercy until he could not speak. He had to stop the fight quick so he could move forward. "I am not going to stop until you are motionless on the ground, and then I am going to drag you into the precinct and hang you up like a pair of dirty underwear," said Bert.

Jay was surprised. *There's insight*, Jay thought to himself; words hurt. He hauled off and hit Bert hard, knocking him across the concrete. The crack of his jaw could be heard from inside the house, but Pauline and Jeanna paused only to continue talking after hearing nothing.

Inside Pauline and Jeanna had hit it off, in contrast to their men. They were talking about different things while Breanna and Heather chatted between themselves, unintentionally imitating their mom's and Pauline's conversation. They had eaten practically all the hummus and most of the shrimp that Jeanna had set down on the island. Jeanna sent them to play in the family room.

"Jeanna, it's not always going to be so bad," said Pauline. "I hear other moms talk about it all the time in our women's groups. The trick is not to let your circumstances dictate your relationship. Get a counselor, and if you don't mind me saying, get a life. Life gets hard when you center it around other people, no matter who they are in relation to you. Love them, love God first, but love them as you love yourself. You need to be okay with you, honest and true with your values. Not sure if you're Christian, but it still is true whether you or not." Jeanna liked Pauline and had misjudged her. She did not picture her as the direct type.

Outside the house, Jay and Bert continued to fight. As Jay had promised himself, he was having fun, but as soon as the fun ended, he would have to reach deep inside himself and turn off a switch. It was a switch for which he was in therapy most of his life. "Truce. I need to get this off my chest," he said before playtime was truly over.

Punches were still thrown. Bert shook off his comment like a dog shaking off water. "Not even if you surrender. I don't trust you that you won't get back up again." He tried to get Jay in a choke hold, but Jay would not surrender. The more they fought, the more aggravated they became and aggressively agitated. Jay wanted to finish his apology, and Bert yearned for him to stop speaking.

The old school drop and lock did not work. "What was that about dirty underwear, your mamma?" asked Jay, regaining his composure and footing. The anger was unrequited, and Jay had to stop. Either he took a hit which would be too hard for him to ignore—tempting, he thought; after all, he did call for a truce—or he would maneuver, taking less of a hit to some other part of the body.

"Truce, you have to quit!", he said again. "I was working with the FBI, gathering intel for them against Jaks and trying to source out the company from these organizations. That's how we knew the funding was multifaceted, almost taking on a life of its own. It was not just drugs. It was trafficking, in ways that made me sick. I have daughters and hopefully a son someday. We're trying. Thinking about it in the office made me puke and puke again." He kept dodging Bert's fist. He wondered when his words would sink into his big fat head.

It was wound up and ready to go when Bert finally heard Jay's words. It was impossible for him to stop, except for God's hand, but the punch stopped in midair. "That's what happened?" asked Bert.

Jay looked at his fist. He had no idea how his fist did not land on his skull, but was glad as Jeanna and Pauline walked outside onto the deck to see what was causing the commotion. Their collective mouths were agape. "Sorry," Jay said. He put his bloody fist behind his back.

Both detectives were looking rough. Bert had a little more respect for his less than equal, younger, and less clever partner. He laughed to himself but felt pain. "Jay and I were just testing each other's reflexes, sparring. Jay, you have quick moves," said Bert, so relieved there was no betrayal that he wanted to cry.

Pauline knew it to be a drag-out brawl. She covered her mouth and shook her head.

Bert was no longer concerned about appearances. "You couldn't have said something to me over coffee?" he asked. The data added up quickly; he could not talk about the facts since it was still confidential. Jay already had clearances, so he could work that angle for the FBI. *Heck, he's probably an agent*, thought Bert. "Oh, that is a tangled web," he said. Neither of them wanted to say too much about the situation in front of the women.

The vegetables were done. Jay quickly removed them from the grill and put on the steaks. He told Jeanna to watch them, approximately four minutes on each side for medium well. They both went to clean up. Bert borrowed an old T-shirt of Jay's. By the time they had finished washing up, the kitchen table was prepared with everything on it.

They blessed their food. "Hey, isn't that one of Daddy's T-shirts that Uncle Bert is wearing?" asked Breanna. Pauline did not know what to think.

Jeanna was at a loss as well, but was good at quick rebuttals. She told her, "Friends like to borrow friends' clothes like you and Heather do as sisters." She then gave Jay a dirty look. Breanna thought about it and shook her head in agreement as she took her fork and put a green bean in her mouth. Heather looked confused as she did not ever remember borrowing any piece of clothing from her older sister. Unsatisfied, she refused to eat.

The evening ended early, and Pauline and Bert left right after dinner. The car ride was long and quiet. "Do you want to talk about it?" Bert asked. He realized it should have been the other way around. It should have been Pauline who was concerned with what happened, but as it was if Pauline had gotten the revelation that she was marrying a cop. There was a heaviness that set on her heart, but she had been praying for him since the day she met him, and he was okay. He would be okay again and again.

She started to cry; she did not want Bert to see it, but he knew. He held her hand for the car ride home. "It's what I do for a living that's bothering you, right?" he asked. She did not respond. "It requires sacrifices. I am sorry about tonight. That should not have happened, a communications glitch. But know this: what I do, I do for God, our city, state and now country and for you."

Chapter Nine

The Tide

It was another Saturday. Hudson no longer felt safe anywhere. He was able to smuggle himself off the island in a small boat. He left immediately after he met with Captain Jaks. He had a double come to the island and take his place at the hotel that night and go to the airport in the morning. He was pretty sure he was going to get shot either going to the airport or getting on the plane. He was later surprised to find out that his double made it home safely.

The small boat, after about ten hours of sailing, met with a medium-size yacht. He paid a sum up front and then promised he would give them the rest of their money once he safely reached his destination. The sailors were rewarded generously for stowing him. While he lay in the cabin sleeping, they discussed what they would do if somehow he forgot to pay them. They had a good laugh when he gave them the money.

At five knots the yacht was able to make up for time lost. Hudson needed to be at the destination island by two PM. They sailed about another thirty miles. At noon they docked at Cook's Island only long enough for Hudson to obtain a passport and US ID. He boarded the cruise ship as a passenger named John Hudson. He was pleased, not because the passenger had his last name as his first name or because he was still alive, but he was back in the game.

The alias was new. It was untraceable to any of his other identities. He had paid half his savings for his escape, but he could start again anywhere. John Hudson originated his cruise in Australia so that was the destination. John Hudson was a New Yorker who took an extended leave of absence from his job over sixteen months ago. New York, who would have thought? Eventually he would be going back to New York, his birthplace, to get lost in the big city. There he would blend like a chameleon with a new background and new underground network of connections. Once again he would play in the shadows of the Big Apple where it all started, but as for this Saturday he was in Australia.

The Bureau was doubly surprised that they had been given the shake by someone who was no cleverer than a common burglar. The map of his past whereabouts were lit up with small dots. Now they had a photo and prints, things were popping up internationally as well as within the United States. The Hudson case no longer belonged to the new detectives but to the CIA and other international organizations. The DC, Jay, and Bert were glad to be rid of him and knew that by and by, they would catch their guy.

The conference was getting busier as more agencies were moving into the top floor. The DC, Jay, and Bert entered the conference room to find yellow folders in designated spots on the table next to coffees from Starbucks. The DC had told Sara that she didn't need to do that, but she said she stopped for coffee anyway. There was also a box of tissues in the middle of the table.

The information was passed around about the second person who had prints at the murder scene and also at the den with the detonator. "We still know nothing about him," said the DC, "except that he's on our side. Apparently, he missed two hits that he was supposed to take for the company and is also willing to give us information in exchange for partial freedom and protection for his family. He also changed the detonator settings so it would not go off. We have not accounted for the prints at the murder scene, but we believe he was not there at the time of murder was committed. Anyway, he is cooperating with the federal authorities. So the gaps are being closed quickly."

The folders were all opened and everyone had questions. "Hurray for our side," said Sara, raising a fist in the air. "It's always good to have a little victory when it comes to justice." Everyone agreed with her, and they raised their coffee cups.

***

The morning started at five AM. Pauline could not sleep. Something did not sit right. It was possible it was Bert, but she was not sure. That was how the subconscious worked. Secrets sometimes were unfolded in dreams. She opened her Bible and read and prayed, as she communed with the Lord. The Lord was moving mountains; she just could not see it, but she trusted Him for it. If she could not sleep, it was for a good reason. It was just that most of the time she did not know what it was or why it was, but once God gave her peace, she was okay to fall back to sleep.

Psalms was the book in the Bible that she had Alexa read to her at night, and it never failed to help her get to sleep. It was listening to God's truths that calmed her anxious thoughts. Tonight it was Ecclesiastes 9. It talked about marriage and living life and doing the best you can do at whatever you are doing. The sentiment was that you have one breath and that you need to live life to the fullest, for death will come; so do your best as unto the Lord. It was what she needed to read. It was okay to get married to Bert, *And when I commit to something, I will give it everything I have, because I only have one breath and one life by God's grace,* she thought. *I think that is right. To choose life and to go forward the best you can no matter what the circumstances are that you face. In God's grace there is mercy, so pray.*

The peace came, and she was able to go back to sleep. The next morning was going to be a lot of writing and coffee. Her routine had become predictable, other than morning visitors. Other people might have found it boring, but she liked it. She was midway in her story with Kara and Naomi. They found each other finally by the grace of God.

> Kara and Naomi were on the path back home when the thick gray smoke started to come their way. It could not be averted. They quickly turned around and walked in the opposite direction. They covered their faces and their eyes with shirts. Kara prayed and asked Naomi if she wanted to pray as well. She said yes, but they would have to walk quick and pray as the wind was blowing in different directions. "Lord, please make the smoke and fire stop if it is Your will," asked Kara. Naomi asked why she added "if it was His will," if she did not know what God's will was. "It's obvious, isn't it? God's will is best. We don't know what it looks like from up there, from where we stand, our sight is limited." They both looked up, and the winds died down. She held her sister's hand once more. It was that for which she was most grateful.

The worship music was loud. She sang at the top of her lungs for no one to hear. She sat in the kitchen and worked on her monthly obligations. She had given up typing and story writing until tomorrow and she would start again. She worked diligently on her finances, but to no avail. She still would be a little short this month for the upgrade on the coffee machine she wanted. She went on to do her email and then the invites for Sammie's wedding. They had argued back-and-forth about who was responsible for the invites. Pauline insisted that the bride sends out her own invites to her own wedding, but Sam said Mia would do it.

It was exhausting. She gave in and said she would do the invites for Sam. After she finished her emails and her finances, she would start on the invites. Sam told Pauline to only use calligraphy, but she said no way. She did not even want to handwrite the invitations but knew that was how she would want it done. Payback was coming, she thought. Sam wanted to send them to all the people who had already responded with a no, but Pauline said that was out of the question and desperate. If she had extra room, she could invite those who had children, their children, but Sammie did not want any children at her wedding. It would be too hard to move around them. Little did she know that later on in life she would not have one child but seven of her own.

The afternoon quickly advanced into mid-afternoon. Pauline was only on her fifteenth invitation when there was a knock on the door and someone talking into her intercom. It was Charlie and Lucy. They were holding hands. She tried not to look too smug, but she could not hide it. *I told you so* was the only thing that came to mind, so she said it.

The romance of the young sells, but at last she wrote a different genre. She invited them into her home with open arms. They all hugged. "Well look at you two. I'm not one for 'I told you so,' but I told you so. Would you guys like something to eat?" Charlie held up a bag of chicken, biscuits, coleslaw and potatoes. Anyone did not want Pauline to go to the trouble.

They followed Pauline into the kitchen and set the food on the table. Pauline had the paper plates from the pantry beside the food by time they were seated at the table. She also went and retrieved the silverware and set it out next to the plates. Charlie had already helped himself to a pitcher of half tea and half lemonade. "So when did you stop doing cans?" he asked. Pauline explained that she went back and forth between the two and stocked up in the pantry in case he had a preference. He said he liked the homemade stuff the best and looked at Lucy like she should be taking notes.

Young love is blind. Lucy smiled and shook her head in agreement; she had a lovesick look on her face. Pauline on the other hand could not help but notice the naïveté. She could not help but think it was after the first few years that real love sets into a relationship. You have had your first dozen fights and you are no longer walking on eggshells to please each other. You are comfortable but not too comfortable.

The lights illuminated the front and the back yard. It had been advanced to an auto-setting to turn on at dusk. She could ask Alexa to turn it off, which she did normally since her electricity bill was running a little high, but since today was a special occasion, and she had guests, she kept the lights lit. "So to what do I owe this unexpected pleasure?" asked Pauline.

There is a difference. They looked at each other and then looked at Pauline and then back at each other. Charlie nodded yes. Lucy showed Pauline her ring. "Isn't it great?" she said. "I was unsure about everything, even God, but I am a believer now. I accepted the Lord before Charlie and I ever started dating.

The conscience can be your true north. My conscience had been eating at me for some time, and I understood who Jesus was I just did not want to be a Christian, but the alternative was that I could no longer live with myself. Even the smallest of sins craved forgiveness, so I surrendered. I had nothing left to lose. It was either become a zombie and drink the Kool-Aid, or live and die in my sins. I said yes to Jesus and I realized that I was a zombie after-all. She laughed.

Pauline's eyes widened. She was not sure about the analogy. She only knew that being a Christian was not like either of those things and told her so.

The lights were appropriate. It was a time to celebrate. She gave Lucy a kiss and a hug and included Charlie again in the hug. She then went to get a bottle of sparkling cider from the pantry. "Try not to say too much at church," said Charlie. "We still need to talk to the pastor together. He knew that I was going to ask Lucy but doesn't know I did. We wanted you to be the first to know."

Pauline was happy for them—and herself, as she too was secretly engaged.

★★★

All was in rebellion. The company, Tabs, needed a lead person and had none. No-one would step up. All the corporate heads who wanted change, both as reforms for social justice as well as for states to secede from the United States, had not only withdrawn funding but gone back into the shadows. As the infrastructure started to collapse, no one wanted to be associated with the company. Tabs tried to rally reform by staging other events and demonstrations, stirring up different groups, but communities had had enough and no longer would be manipulated.

Tabs had everyone in place, yet none of their intel was accurate. The move was supposed to happen before the new agency ever came into existence. It was slated over six months ago for Bert and Jay to become new federal agents with access to files that would start to make sense only to officers that had worked the streets. The network that connected the drugs, trafficking, and criminal protesting was easy pinpoint for them from the streets if given enough time and testimony.

It was a game of connect-the-dots, not just between local criminal activity but also that of state- and government-run organizations. It was a small difference. It was about communication across not only state lines but also the departmental staff. As originators of Tabs convened via Zoom, they pointed fingers at each other and made accusations. They were losing their backing for reform. It was in this city they had planned their first overthrow of government, and nothing went right. The officers that were supposed to be removed from the system were promoted and given clearances as they spoke.

★★★

The conference room was filled. Instead of three, there were now fifteen people, not including Detective Captain Murphy. They all had coffee in hand except for Sara; she was standing at the coffee machine helping herself to an espresso. Captain Murphy handed everyone an orange folder with the latest details on the company they now knew as Tabs. It was known for terrorist activities but no one knew how deep the roots of the organization went.

The tide had turned. The department and the agency were on the offensive for once. The new board showed lights and dots that now could be connected via informant or intel. Interstate departments were sharing information, and arrests were being made on a large scale across state lines and city lines. The police, with the help of concerned citizens, were able to target those who were targeting officials and others. Even within the gangs, officials were able to get members to turn state's evidence against drug lords.

The communities were being inundated with groups that no longer tolerated the lack of education and subpar living conditions. Private and state funding was available for institutions that would work at cost in different parts of the communities trying to establish better human developmental standards. It started with the simplest staples, like clean drinking water.

It ended with safe communities, access to educational assistance and help providers. Employment was more about setting up equipment from their homes and securing free internet access so that a job could be sourced for them.

The company was still around but not as big and not as strong as it had been in the past. No one supported an invisible cost. The government converted back to its legislative ways. If you wanted something changed it had to go through the House and the Senate. The only thing that was changing was the unity and cohesiveness of the states. Their enforcement was now at a national level as well as a local level. The officers were being held to a higher standard where they no longer were able to hide state evidence. Drugs were no longer stored but destroyed.

Dispatchers were now vetted and federally certified, not just trained on the state systems with a federal repository database of calls.

The room had many new faces. Every week they had a new face. The institution within a few months had done so well that other states were asking to model the institution, but since it was federally run, the template was not accessible to state governments only but those who would abide by the same federal mandates. They sat around the table and took stabs at what local institutions were being shut down for illegal activities and which institutions needed protection from criminal activity. They also were backup for the police, as many came from the force.

★★★

The FBI had gathered in Washington DC to discuss the new organization. It was part of the discussion as to whether they would include some of the operatives who had been working out in the field with ex-military or military experience. Only Jay, Bert, and the DC were a part of the conversation. It was of the opinion that having mercenaries or operatives aboard would damage the new organization's reputation.

The room was smaller than most, but it was the perfect size for the eight of them. "I want to introduce you to Agent Coaster," said Agent Becks. The seven-by-ten screen showed a man with his family. "He had no intel on the company but was hired by the company. His alias was Derby. No one saw him, but yet he dodged three attempts on lives that have been able to help us establish who Tabs is and all the institutions to which they are connected. Anyone want to guess who he is?"

The agent conducted the meeting as if they were back in the investigation room. "It's man number two. He's the one who changed the detonation for the two civilians, Treble and Stern, who will testify against Hudson. The next would-be Jaks and Bert, is my guess," said Jay.

Agent Becks shook his head as if he was a professor pleased with his student's answer and pointed to his nose. "He works only for us now. He had worked as an operative in the past for us but changed sides and now is back. It would be good if he worked directly with the new organization," said Agent Becks.

The hairs on the back of Bert's neck stood up once again. It could be a double-cross, perhaps a last attempt to get things moving in a different direction for Tabs. Too many people had gone down within the outer rim, and they no longer had funding. They were grabbing at straws. "Bring him in," said Bert, "but I am sure as heck going to arrest him. That son of gun has a criminal history a mile long. I'll forgive him, but he's going down along with whatever money laundering organization he works for."

Derby took the earbuds out of his ears and put them in his pocket. He could defend himself but Bert was right. He was dirty, and he would turn again for the right price, but living the government constructs gave him the structure he needed for his two little girls to grow up in one place. He knocked on the door of the conference room.

The door opened, and Agent Becks welcomed Agent Coaster into the meeting. "Hi, I'm Coaster. I've been listening—and yes, I can do that, it's allowed. Don't pick up your stones yet. Let me tell you how I can assist and not interfere with operations. Use me as an operative to think like an operative and to engage as an operative. I am a patriot. I have listed every crime I have committed, and none have been against the government. The other operations are at a higher classification. It's why I have the clearances I do and was able to listen in on this meeting."

He turned to Bert. "We need people like you, Bert, who can sniff out people like me. Man," he said and opened the file he had in his hand and looked at his contribution in arrests and case files on which he assisted, "you are something from a Marvel comic book. And you, Jay—well, we've met in a previous life."

The instinct was to stand in front of Jay. He would take a bullet for his partner. "Bad blood," said Bert, "has to go through me first."

Agent Becks thought to interrupt, but he did not know which side he would be on. "Jay?"

They were brothers. "War is hell. Murder is war. Wrong is murder.", said Jay. He knew Coaster from the military. They had worked closely beside each other on one project, but his profile told a different story. He went in and got the bad guy. One operation after another, after another, lives were saved, but reputations got jaded, and the politics were asphyxiating.

Bert was already standing in front of Jay, who had stood as well. He grabbed Bert by the side of the neck. "It's okay, we're all in it together."

Coaster stepped forward as did Jay. They shook hands. "Hudson, do you remember?" asked Coaster. Jay shook his head. "He was the operative they used in Baghdad. It was later that he went rogue. I'll be able to track him back to the US so he can be arrested. He always comes back to the US and he wants not only viability again but revenge. He doesn't care how he gets it or many lives get in the way. He's sloppy now. It's always a sign.", said Derby. Jay looked at the DC, who shook his head no.

Derby/Coaster looked at the DC. "I know CIA, but just so you know. He may be coming this way. I can have your back."

Jay had played his game before with operatives. They almost all flipped. "So what do you get out of this, family and a better vocation?", asked Jay. He nodded. Jay sat back down and opened the orange file.

Coaster took a place at the table, repeating over in his head what Jay had said. *War is hell. Murder is war. Wrong is murder. Where do you go from there?* He wondered if there was any sanity or sanctity to life anymore when the bad guys become good guys, and the good guys become bad guys. He hoped he would never have to take a life again.

His thoughts were interrupted. "Forgot the last line," Jay said. "Love covers a multitude of wrongs." He was thinking about his own life and his need for forgiveness and restoration.

★★★

It was a few months later when Hudson showed up and was arrested. The CIA had tracked him back to New York. It was a fluke; a new recruit was checking the roster of a cruise ship to and from Cook's Island, which had departed the day after he went missing. The passenger had the same name, Hudson. The new recruit had a hunch and cross-referenced it with flights coming into New York. She did a little research, pulled up an image, and bam! One of the most wanted was apprehended. They brought him in and charged him.

Tabs was no more, it had dwindled to nothing. The corruption was sought out and diminished. There were no longer any state statutes that tolerated the harm and destruction of properties, no matter how justified the cause. People stood up for their rights to defend themselves, the choice to worship and praise of all religions, the right to speak freely, and the right to live. The United States stayed united in fundamental principles under God.

Pauline and Bert were early to Sam's wedding. He was her plus-one. Since she was Sam's proxy matron of honor she did not have to be in the ceremony. *It all worked out*, thought Pauline. "Are you glad you came?" she asked Bert, putting her hand on his arm. He said yes as a tear rolled from his eye, and he placed his hand on Pauline's and told her how beautiful she was, which made her blush. She knew how much he loved her and was glad to see his sentimental side. They might be an odd couple, but it worked for both of them.

Soon they both were crying as they watched Sam walk down the aisle. She handed him her handkerchief as she had used his. They had already set a date for their wedding. It would be within the year, and Sam and Lucy were her matrons. Bert had the DC, Jay, and Charlie. She was on the spot for one more matron, but who would be her plus-one? Mia, she thought, but then who would be her proxy. After the wedding they went to Jay's and Jeanna's house to help them move.

It was late Sunday when they arrived. Boxes were neatly stacked in the garage and each of the other rooms. The girls had been put to bed. Jeanna had her Love radio station on and was dancing and listening to Toby as she packed her boxes. "We have a great God, don't we?" Jeanna said. Pauline nodded in agreement. It was never too late or early for a little praise and worship, she thought.

Jay could count on one phone call every Sunday. "Hey man, what's up?" asked Jay. Whether it was interrupting a ball game or a Sunday dinner, he was open for the call. Sometimes it was a visit. He would just come over and a watch a game with him.

Pascal was reconsidering his major. He wanted to graduate with a criminal justice degree and go into the agency, but he was not sure. It was either that or get his juris doctorate. Either way, it was another two years. He would have to go into the policy academy for two years, which seemed like a long time on top of finishing his degree or law school, which was more expensive.

The call was the same, something was always up. "Well, it's like this," Pascal said. "My friend, or actually a friend of a friend needs some advice. He was charged with possession, but it was less than a gram. What should he do?" Jay would cut in and ask him what he thought. "He did the crime, but it's his first misdemeanor, not even a traffic violation. I'm not sure."

Jay asked him for his friend's information. He said he would look into it for him which he did.

Printed in the United States
by Baker & Taylor Publisher Services